FRENCH PAINTING

THE BOX AT THE THEATRE *By Pierre-August Renoir* (1841-1919)

FRENCH PAINTING

T. W. EARP

WITH 44 ILLUSTRATIONS IN COLOUR AND MONOCHROME

AVALON PRESS AND
CENTRAL INSTITUTE OF ART AND DESIGN

"Discussions on Art"

Already Published

BRITISH PAINTING (*From Hogarth's Day to Ours*) by William Gaunt
ITALIAN PAINTING (*Up to Leonardo and Raphael*) by Tancred Borenius
FRENCH PAINTING by T. W. Earp

Forthcoming

ITALIAN PAINTING (*From Titian onward*)
DUTCH PAINTING
FLEMISH PAINTING
SPANISH PAINTING
AMERICAN PAINTING

Each volume in crown quarto, with from 32 to 44 full-page
Plates in Colour and Monochrome

Produced by Avalon Press, Ltd., London—by arrangement with
Central Institute of Art and Design
1945

TEXT PRINTED IN GREAT BRITAIN BY RICHARD CLAY AND COMPANY, LTD., BUNGAY
COLOUR PLATES BY HENRY STONE & SON, LTD., BANBURY, AND GEORGE PULMAN &
SON, LTD., WEALDSTONE. PHOTOGRAVURE BY HARRISON & SONS, LTD., HIGH WYCOMBE

FRENCH PAINTING

I. CLASSIC AND ROMANTIC

VOLTAIRE, who collected pictures and sometimes dealt in them, wrote that French painting began with Nicolas Poussin † (1594–1665) in the reign of Louis XIII. It was the statement of an 18th-century connoisseur, ignorant of his country's Primitives, or counting them beneath notice as Gothic and barbarous. Yet in a qualified way it was true, for Poussin is the first French painter on whom his successors to the present day have looked back as a living influence. He stands at the head of the current of modern French art, and Cézanne, who for us renewed its vigour, said that it was necessary " to do Poussin again from nature ".

The history of art is a sequence of violent reactions and impetuous returns; Poussin reacted against the Renaissance. François I, when he invaded Italy, had been caught in the ardour of the new paganism, with its revelation of Greek legend as a treasure of inspiration for the Italian painters. Some of these he invited to France, to decorate the palaces rising at Fontainebleau and on the banks of the Loire, and, incidentally, to end the primitive tradition. For the French painters, following Court fashion, adopted the Italian style. Throughout the disturbed rule of the House of Valois, such art as civil war permitted to emerge was tinged with the Renaissance spirit, though the first high temperature of the movement gradually chilled. When Poussin appeared, the Greek revival, so far as painting was concerned, had become an empty but tyrannical convention, and though he also went to antiquity, he made his own discovery of it.

The artists of the French renaissance had tinged their representation of the ancient

† Plate 5

world with the sentiments of contemporary gallantry. Poussin pierced through their luscious ornament and superficial sugariness to formulate a sterner version of the fabulous age—one in keeping with the gravity of his own temperament, and symptomatic, too, of changing ideas in France. For after a long period of anarchy Richelieu had begun his labour of giving unity to the realm, not only reducing the feudal power of the great nobles, but establishing Paris more firmly as a capital. There, his official patronage gave to art and literature an echo of his own consolidating efforts; they took on a new moral tone which corresponded with his programme of political reform. A sense of order, and an evocation of the virtues rather than the voluptuousness of antiquity, possessed the creative imagination. They found rhetorical expression in the plays of Corneille, based on the dramatic unities of time and place, redolent of Roman heroism and austerity, and pictorial expression in the works of Poussin.

Although Poussin spent most of his painting life in Rome, his pictures retained this imprint of France at the beginning of the 17th century. Contemporary Italian painting left him unattracted by the forced drama of its emphatic light and shade and its exaggeration of sentiment and gesture. His essentially native qualities of reason and realism, evident in the deliberate balance of his design and his fidelity to the elements of nature, however fancifully he might blend them, never ceased their restraint. And though the restraint might brim with feeling, it did not break into disorder.

In this respect he found himself in complete

sympathy with one Italian predecessor. For poise in emotion and execution alike, Raphael set him a constant example. From him Poussin drew his science. But he kept for his own those parts of the painting which reveal the artist's individual temperament and are the first things to disappear from the canvas of one who only imitates. Poussin's light was deeper than Raphael's, his colour more clamorous, and his detail sharper.

Another influence adopted by him from Italy, which flaws the entire production of the classical school, was Greek and Roman sculpture, with its canon of the ideal human figure and its curriculum of standardised gesture. Each art has its own principles, which it is a fallacy to transfer to another. The convention of perfect beauty, however applicable to one kind of sculpture, imposes a limitation on painting, which, apart from the abstract picture, seeks especially to give the illusion of life and nature in all their variety. Poussin's study of ancient statues tended to generalise, and so weaken the expressiveness of his figures; and the same fault, from the same cause, appears in his followers.

Yet it is only a little way that he asks us to go with him in the pursuit of sculpturesque form, and his reconstruction of mythology is the most convincing that painting has known. His gods and goddesses, his nymphs and satyrs, are pictorially credible. They move in a setting pieced together from a diversity of studies from nature, yet coherent and wonderfully evocative of its denizens. And though his design is most frequently divided into two corresponding halves, the lively intricacy within these halves, and the rhythmic connection of the figures, give a quickening heat of life to the ruling symmetry. The colour, if a little raw, brings vividness; and a recurrent strain of intense blue is peculiarly Poussin's. His light is usually that of a late golden afternoon, serene and serious. In his religious subjects the rhythm is slower, and the pensive mood more stressed. His landscapes guard the same mellow solemnity; there is a mature enchantment, a cadence, in their wildness of mountain and valley. Few painters have revealed such depth of imagination with such clarity of statement as Poussin.

A friend of his in Rome was his fellow-countryman and fellow-artist Claude Gellée, better known, from the region of his birth, as Claude Lorrain † (1600–1682). He, too, spent the greater part of his life in what was then the painter's city, where he first arrived at the age of thirteen. Employed by the painter Tassi as servant and pupil, he turned to the exclusive practice of landscape, in which he was greatly influenced by another foreign settler in Rome, the German Elsheimer. But while the shapes and arrangement of his scenes show little inventive power of his own, and easily lapsed into a mechanical formula, his manner of bathing them in a clear suffusion of light brought something new into art. Here he was the ancestor of our own Turner, and, through him, of the Impressionist school.

It might, indeed, be said that Claude had only one subject, and that it was the light as he knew it sometimes in his wanderings on the Roman Campagna, at its most luminous hours of dawn or sunset. The immediate themes of his pictures are of little consequence. Almost invariably they conform to the same design of a horizontal between two verticals. In the middle is a level of sea or plain, bounded on either side by rising ground or an architectural fantasy of palace or temple, hardly attempting more than pasteboard consistency. Minor accessories of figures or animals are under-laboured or over-laboured, while the ships which add perfunctory interest to the marine pieces are purely decorative constructions, unsubstantial as the trees of the landscapes. But the light that caresses the rudimentary plan dissolves this half-conveyed reality and transforms it into the dream of an unsullied day. The mood is impersonal, its completion eked out by the scenic contrivances of the theatre,

† Plate 6

which fulfil the needs of the classical conception. Yet Claude's instinct, triumphant where calculation could hardly have succeeded, attains its effect. He captures the impalpable, the radiance of a sunlit Golden Age.

In the imaginary architecture of towers and columns, and in the visionary approach to the past, which drew upon the symbolism and sentiment of his time, Claude shows his only adherence to a period and a school. Antoine Watteau † (1684–1721), alone among French painters Claude's equal in poetic suggestion, sprang directly from his own age and environment—France under Louis XV, when the supremacy of the classical school was challenged by new means of expressing an altered mode of life.

The authority of the Greeks and Romans had waned; they ceased to set the pattern for conduct and taste. France turned back to live in the here and now, gathering from actual existence a moral and artistic impulse whose keynote was relief at the close of the last austere phase of the rule of Louis XIV. The fire that was dying in tragedy revived in comedy, and gallant intrigue supplanted the discussion of the philosophy of Descartes or the heresy of Jansenism as a pastime for the noble and moneyed classes which it was the artists' business to please.

Watteau was the servant of that easy-living section of society which demanded of painting that it should furnish a seductive reflection of its own manners. Born at Valenciennes near the Flemish border, he was encouraged by acquaintance with Flemish art to dwell on detail and on the spectacle of contemporary life. Coming to Paris, he studied with Gillot, whose chief work was the design of theatrical scenery and costumes. Thus his first steps tended towards the depiction of reality, but reality invested with an atmosphere of masquerade. He painted some pictures of military life which gave to the ardours of the campaign an air of agreeable vagabondage. And gradually he dis-

† Plate 7

covered in the Paris collections the masters whose example, in spirit as in method of technique, supported his own inclination. These were Rubens and the Venetians. He copied, indeed, some works of Titian in a patron's collection. By these preferences, and the style into which he welded them, the romantic movement can claim him as one of its precursors. Although it was not done combatively, but for his own purpose, he introduced into French painting the strain that was to run counter to the classical idols—Rubens instead of Raphael, the Venetians instead of the Florentines, and study from the life without an appeal to Greek sculpture for its correction.

In this last respect he was an impassioned realist, for he gave to the most delicate nuances of gesture a psychological intention. The whole muted drama of his personages lies in their attitudes. It seems at first as though they could have no other object than to exist in themselves upon the canvas; but in the manner of their grouping, and, within the groups, in the particular poise of their turning towards each other, the pitch of relationships is exactly registered. And, as the vivacious rhythm of these groups weaves into the more tempered but controlling pulse of the scheme as a whole, all this interplay is caught up in a more general business shared together—a concert, a picnic, or an embarkation for Cythera, the legendary island of delight. Pleasure is the occupation of Watteau's pictured world. Yet its quality is so tremulous, and its seekers so refine upon it, that their exquisite company crosses the verge of possibility to enter a realm of fairyland. To make the sense of illusion more compelling, there sometimes mingle with them the quaintly-vestured figurants of the Italian harlequinade. Starting from the closest fidelity to life, netted in such intimate detail as a hardly-conscious movement or a swift shimmer of bright silk, Watteau with touch after touch evolves a purely visionary conception. No other painter has given such life to artifice, or so completely realised the kingdom of his imagination.

He had many successors in the attempt to satisfy the elegant and leisured hedonism which his own work etherealises. François Boucher (1703–1770), the favourite painter of Mme de Pompadour, confected an infinity of Olympians and shepherds and shepherdesses. They echo the overtones of gallantry in a stylised contemporary-antique mould, insinuating the lesson of Rubens a little more deeply into French art by the way. But their monotonous and metallic glitter claims only deftness of drawing and a feeling for plastic quality. The last of the generation of Watteau, Jean-Honoré Fragonard (1732–1806), approaches nearer to the master, though his manner is more robust and, by comparison, coarse. He is entirely content with externals, but with a swift eye for their pictorial qualities of ready-made values of tone and composition. Those he can seize with rare perception, if not create. There is a fine verve in his brushwork, and his dashing method of attack on the subject is usually brought off by sheer painterly ability. At his best when least elaborate and in whole-hearted surrender to the thing seen, he expresses the spirit of the time, not by psychological insight, but by a wonderful aptitude for letting the surface fact make its full complement of suggestion and formal charm.

While the school of Watteau continued, without his genius, to provide an appropriate system of the picturesque which responded to the taste and pursuits of the aristocracy and the newly-risen clan of finance, Jean-Baptiste Chardin † (1699–1779) was quietly following his own independent course. Confining himself for subject-matter to the life of the little bourgeois, he was the first to transfer successfully to French painting the domesticity of the Dutch masters. To-day he would be called an Intimist for the loving perception with which he displayed the interiors and the household events of the class

† Colour Plate 2 and Plate 8

to which he belonged. But the record of his perception, though sympathetic, was unsentimental in its truth. The children of the house provide many of his themes, but there is nothing mawkish in his presentation of them; a perfect rightness characterises his treatment. What he might have done, so far as sentiment is concerned, had he not refused all concessions to dramatic falsity and the appeal of the obviously attractive, is lamentably shown by Greuze (1725–1805) the contemporary of his later years, who surrendered himself to extracting affecting anecdote and a deceptively innocent prettiness from scenes of rustic life.

Chardin was content with portraying a limited milieu exactly as it stood before him. What must have been a delightful temperament leaves a plain enough imprint on his work, but he never consciously intervenes between the spectator and the picture. And, triumphant as he is in his depiction, he is an artist whose painting in the end is less important for the success of its representation than for the consummate mastery of its craft. The consistency and application of the paint itself, and the compounding of recondite gradations of colour—the very processes of the studio—produce their own large share in the pleasure of Chardin's work. This is especially evident where the human distraction has no part in the enjoyment, in his still-lifes, where another phase of their painter's science is revealed.

For the still-life, as imported from Holland and until practised by Chardin, had won interest by the degree of skill with which the appearance of the objects that built it up was imitated, and to some extent also by the lusciousness or profusion or oddity of those objects. With Chardin the portrayal of the elements of his still-life was not of more account than the design into which they composed and the resources which they offered for the invention of relations in colour. He founded the modern treatment of this fascinating but very overworked branch of art.

Thus, before the Revolution, French painting was following directions with which its later development is linked; but as the political prospect grew darker, the artists' activities were curtailed. The sections of society which had furnished them with patrons were dissolved; the subjects and sentiments which most of them illustrated were out of harmony with the new spirit of the times. But the classical school, whose style was falling into the decline of an academic convention, revived, and at the hands of Louis David overswept all competition.

David † (1748–1825), a great-nephew of Boucher, began by painting in the same rococo manner, but his master Vieu, who was much influenced by the engravings of antique gems, turned him towards a more serious course. This conformed to the fashion for ancient Greece and Rome, which was stimulated by the liberal writers who saw in them the model for a new France. When David, already imbued with their doctrines, visited Rome, it was the atmosphere of its early grandeur that he breathed, while the recent discovery of Herculanaeum and its frescoes seemed to him a closer contact with his political and artistic ideals. Another sustaining nurture for the latter was, as in Poussin's case, classical sculpture; and he went further than Poussin in transferring its canons to his painting. He admired the Italian masters in a lesser degree, though he found support, both in theory and performance, from Michelangelo.

During his residence in Rome as a member of the French School there, of which Vieu was director, he chose as subjects for two huge pictures *The Oath of the Horatii* and *Brutus Condemning his Son*, in which painting was turned from entertainment to propaganda. In their hard relief and stark rigidity of sculpturesque form, these works pushed the constant principle of classicism to its extreme, but their reception, when placed on view in Paris, was enthusiastic.

† Plate 9

They told their story plainly, and celebrated the sterner republican virtues.

That was enough for David to be acclaimed a master, and he became, indeed, as much a dictator in the world of art as his friend Robespierre was in that of politics. His authority lasted longer. A member of the National Convention, he voted for the death of Louis XVI and approved the Terror. He also brought about the abolition of the Royal Academy and of privileged rights of showing in the annual official Salon. Yet only artists of proved revolutionary persuasion were to be allowed to exhibit. With the fall of Robespierre, he narrowly escaped death, and made a recantation of his ardours as a tribune of the people. Retiring to complete his *Intervention of the Sabine Women*, he emerged as Court painter to Napoleon, who greatly appreciated his abilities. The return of the Bourbons brought him under the law of exile for regicide, and he ended his career in Brussels.

In the activity of his life outside the studio he differed from most French painters. Had it not been for the way in which he resolutely occupied the public stage, it is doubtful whether he would have succeeded in placing himself so authoritatively at the head of French painting and in imposing his work as an example to be followed by a succeeding generation. There is a real merit of clear line and characterisation in his portraits, but, shorn of its contemporary relevance, the particular form of classicism in which he was an innovator, like the pictures of state ceremonies undertaken for Napoleon, gives little more than a tireless precision. Their sculpturesque properties endow his figures with a quality of relief, though they suggest less the purity of the sister-art than the waxwork. They gesture, each in its own void on the canvas, joined in no chain of coherent design, and their tint is cadaveric. While they assert the nobility of their artist's conception, and an implacable logic in the way in which he carried it out, they prove also that though painting may progress from crafts-manship to the expression of ideas, movement in the opposite direction is beset with danger.

It was unhappily characteristic that when his pupils asked David for technical advice, he bade them read their Plutarch. Yet one of them, Dominique Ingres † (1780–1867), profited as much as was possible from such instruction, and Ingres is perhaps the best case that can be made out for David. He went to antiquity, but to its poetry and not its politics. He studied its sculpture with intense admiration, but this influence, though it had its baneful result, was largely offset by an equal devotion to Raphael. Ingres pro-ceeded, in fact, through the obligatory syllabus of training for the classical school. He was saved from becoming the standard-ised product by a natural gift for drawing and the realisation that painting ultimately is an art with mechanics of its own, however much literature might affect its subject-matter and sculpture its individual details.

A man of passion beneath an impassive exterior, Ingres gave something of this character of fire beneath the glacier to his work. He did not limit himself to the dic-tionary of mythology in the choice of subjects for his imaginative pictures; in their list are such titles as *Henry IV and his Children*, *Odalisque* and *The Liberation of Angelica*, which would seem by rights the property of the romantics. But when Ingres handles them, they fall into the classical mould as surely as *Oedipus and the Sphinx* or *Stratonice*. They lose their suggestion of excitement and quick action to become ordered and immobile. Whatever the subject, these qualities remain, and Ingres at his best makes a merit of them. For though there is not motion, or only arrested motion, there is, thanks to the marvel of sensitive line and the intellectual force of composition, the illusion of life. The figures do not stir, yet a pulse beats through them; and though the picture as a whole joins in no context of place or time, implies no continuity beyond the

† Plate 10

canvas, it makes its own integrity, holds the event concentrated in its detached instant, and distributes evenly over all the unflicker-ing throb of emotion. The design is not rhythmic, and is sooner a pattern, yet it is active in the complication of its poise, while another quickening element is the colour.

Ingres has been blamed because his colour is inharmonious, and sometimes this is the case to such an extent that it is hardly possible to believe it unintentional. It is more likely that he was of purpose creating a discord, to give more life by its coruscation to the rigidity of form. In the portraits it especially obtains this effect. One notices that some moderns—Matisse and Picasso in certain phases, and many abstract painters—adopt this device to bring liveliness to work that has not a strong dynamic content.

Ingres' portraits, indeed, are the final justification of his manner. They demanded none of the exaggerated references to pre-cedent which he occasionally intruded upon the subject-pictures to stress the sense of the historical past. Greek art and Raphael are not visibly quoted, though their essential qualities of reason and completeness preside serenely over the task. To them Ingres joined the suppleness of line with which he expresses volume by contour, and reproduced the most whispered message as to character that feature can give. One feels an over-whelming authority behind his portrayal, and that none of his sitters ever dared inflict on him the common torment of the portrait-painter by quibbling as to likeness. It is the same authority that he showed as an old man, when the legitimate holder of a theatre-stall which Ingres would have preferred to occupy, would feel a tap on the shoulder, with the words, " I am Monsieur Ingres "—and there was nothing for it but to vacate the seat.

This force, which Ingres did not display obviously on the surface of his painting, gained only slow acknowledgement. It was obscured at the start by the theatricality of David's other followers; and, though

Ingres was made director of the French School at Rome and died at the age of eighty-seven laden with civic honours, his supremacy had been continuously challenged by the adherents of the romantic movement under the leadership of Eugène Délacroix † (1798–1863). They openly engaged against David and his successors a warfare which had been foreshadowed by Théodore Géricault ‡ (1791–1824).

Géricault died at the age of thirty-two, before he had time to cast the full weight of his gifts on the side of romanticism, though there is little doubt that he would have grown into one of its chiefs. As things were, he never entirely freed himself from the Davidian manner, diluted examples of which formed the lifelong production of his master Guérin. Géricault kept to the end such elements of it as the taste for the nude and for rhetorical gesture, which were not benefits, and for clear outline and bold relief, which were. But he refused the tyranny of the classical subject, the static attitudes of sculpture, and the idea that the theme, without the design, was enough to knit isolated figures into unity upon the canvas. He believed that contemporary life could evolve its own grand manner and fire it with passion and energy. *The Raft of the " Medusa "*, the only large work that he was able to complete, embodied his theories, yet was not altogether detached from the academic mode. It is in his smaller studies of dramatic incident, of military life, and of horses and horsemanship, that his impetuous nature and urge to innovation are best shown.

His friend Delacroix, whom he deeply influenced, is diffuse by comparison, without the same tautness and menace of explosion. Yet from the beginning he had a clearer sense of direction. Once the years of pupilage were passed, he rapidly discarded the teachings of Guérin, who was his master also. By his interest in the literature and politics of his time, and his friendship with the writers of the romantic school, Delacroix

formulated a clear notion of the aims of the movement, and consciously set out to be its representative in art. In his first Salon exhibit, *Dante's Barque*, he defiantly turned from the classics to the Middle Ages. Later, with *The Barricade*, he commemorated the radical revolution of 1830. From a voyage to Algiers he brought back a series of works which introduced exoticism into French art. These achievements were so many blows aimed at the academic and classical school. With a wide knowledge of European painting, it was Rubens whom he most consulted, and from whom he adapted the restless surge of his design and the fresh glitter of his colour. Some of his crowded canvases, like *The Assassination of the Bishop of Liège* and *The Death of Sardanapalus*, have the rhythmic flow of a broad river ; for his pictures, unlike those of Ingres, are not enclosed upon themselves, but are sections of some wider action whose completion is beyond their limits—a characteristic of Delacroix which the coming Impressionists were frequently to use for the purpose of giving, almost literally, the sense of a slice of life to their work.

Delacroix ransacked history and literature for his subjects. At the time of the battle of Classic *v.* Romantic, the illustrative content of a picture had its importance in view of the classic's desire to restrict it. He took avowed delight in new and strange themes, though he did not let them lead him to neglect the necessity of revolution in painting itself. It is a mistake to consider him preoccupied with the literary element in art ; he appreciated it, but kept it in its place. He introduces a mass of incident and vivid detail, which undoubtedly enlivens the story, but it enlivens and carries on the composition as well. He is a master of the dramatic, with which his portraiture also is usually tinged ; and no painting, once it has stood the test imposed by its own art, is any the worse for offering dramatic interest as well. His classical opponents blamed Delacroix

† Plates 11 and 12   ‡ Plate 13

because in his case the interest was nearer to Shakespeare than to Racine. It was his crime that he revealed new worlds, both in ideas and craftsmanship. To-day they are so well known that we are less apt to credit him with his discoveries. In order justly to do so, it is necessary to put ourselves for a moment in the position of the classic, that we might exclaim as David did, at the sight of *Dante's Barque*: "Where does he come from? I do not know that touch."

II. THE RETURN TO NATURE

DELACROIX was true to appearances, even though they presented themselves only to his imagination; from them he drew the elements of form which composed his picture as a work of art, apart from other extraneous interest. The classic imposed those elements upon the appearances. Delacroix preferred to quicken his whole design with the life of rhythm, rather than to deaden it by making it evenly tip the scales of balance. Both parties conducted the battle more ostensibly around the subject-picture. In landscape, however, by the time that Delacroix issued his challenge, the anti-classical revolt was on the point of breaking out.

For the classical School, though with a weaker grip, possessed nature as well as the human scene. Hubert Robert (1733–1808), whom David worked actively to get imprisoned during the Revolution from a motive that can only have been jealousy, and Joseph Vernet (1714–1789) were the best painters in France of the classical landscape. It descended from Claude, but lacked his saving magic of atmosphere. It depended more on a formal arrangement of mountainous scenery, usually enlivened by a cascade and (to preserve the spirit of antiquity) scattered here and there with ruins. At its best, the recipe gave an unreal but charming decorative effect. It evoked a vision of Italy mingled with a gentle melancholy stirred by its vestiges of crumbled grandeur.

When, during the Revolution and for some time afterwards, war and their own poverty prevented the landscape artists from visiting the scenes from which this kind of picture was compounded, it was not too difficult to do it out of their own heads, though it became more and more detached from reality, approaching rather the conventional painting of China-ware. At the same time, it had the disadvantage of recalling the mode of the *ancien régime*, of being but the empty echo of a dead fashion, and, by its actual decorative properties, bringing to mind a reminiscence of the society that it had been evolved to please. The painters began to look nearer at home for their subjects, and, as the new bourgeois world started its tenacious habit of excursion to the outskirts of Paris in order to enjoy the delights of nature, the region around the capital offered a fresh and appropriate appeal to the picturesque. Yet there was something a little forced about the result. It seems to intimate that the painters were aware of being content with a second-best, that they would still have preferred Italy, and, with its mirage before their eyes, had teased the more homely scene before them into something that it was not. The solution of the difficulty came from England.

The Salon of 1822 brought not only the revelation of *Dante's Barque*, but of the Early English school of water-colourists as well. Bonington † (1802–1828), who was actually living and working in France (he was regarded as a French painter, in fact), Copley, Fielding and Varley showed that, given the eye and the skill, it was not necessary to sigh for Italy to furnish subjects for landscape. Every country, it was demonstrated, had its particular elements of the picturesque if, when

† Plate 14

III. REALISM

COROT and Millet lived and worked away from Paris, detached from the strife of opposed schools of painting and out of touch with contemporary events. Their pictures bear the imprint of no scholastic point of view and of no period, Corot's being concentrated exclusively on the abiding aspects of nature, Millet's overriding particularities with his compelling generalisation. They both died in the early years of the Third Republic, Corot having known six changes in the régime of France, and Millet five. These changes and the social evolution that accompanied them had not left other painters so untouched; while Honoré Daumier † (1808–1879) took an active part in bringing one of them about.

The best part of his existence was consumed in the ceaseless production of drawings for the comic journals, most of which were also organs of political parties. Daumier, himself a strong Radical, did much of his work for *Le Charivari*, a paper on the opposition side, to which he contributed a long series of caricatures attacking King Louis-Philippe and his Government. Savage in their intensity, despite suppression from time to time by the police, they made a deep effect on popular opinion. Yet while his merciless thrusts were appreciated, they were not wholeheartedly enjoyed. Their ruthlessness and the nearness in style of the grotesque to the macabre gave an uneasy shudder. For this refusal to tickle the public palate Daumier never reached high payment, producing his weekly masterpieces for a pittance.

"The fellow has something of Michelangelo under his skin," said Balzac when he saw one of Daumier's caricatures, and Daumier made no secret of the source to which he owed much of his plastic quality and force of line. He gave elasticity to the Michelangelesque design, translating it, as it were, into colloquial idiom, using it as a redoubtable weapon upon innumerable topics.

In his flow of invention, which never ran diluted, it was Balzac himself whom he most resembled; his albums compose a pictorial *Comédie Humaine*. In one series he scourged the classicism of the Davidian school; in another, the machinery of the law; in another, the intrigue of the theatrical profession; and so on, until the France, or at any rate the Paris, of his time, lay dissected in every member by his scarifying analysis. His most mordant severities were directed against the bourgeoisie in general; but for the poor and the unclassed he has a sympathy whose expression is of poignant effect. In his flicks at vagabonds, mountebanks and old broken-down rogues there is something of affection. He assumes no pomposity of moral attitude.

In Daumier's painting, where his sympathies shine with equal clearness but the caricature takes on a darker and more tragic aspect, his master in form is still Michelangelo, though there are reminiscences of Rembrandt in the sudden light and the profundity of shadow. His backgrounds reveal him as one of the most successful interpreters of the spirit of Paris as displayed in its urban landscape, the individuality of the quays and bridges of the Seine, the grey unity of façades and the desolation of outer suburbs, completing the emotional implication of his scene as a whole. Sometimes he adds ferocity to a subject from Molière, sometimes a quaintness to the fantasy of Cervantes, though most of the paintings are contemporary and realistic in theme and treatment.

It was a realism of character and of incident without anecdote. Though it is plain that Daumier could have felt himself in close relationship with his old print-hunters on the quays, his heroic working-women or his carriage full of third-class passengers, he does not arrange his facts into a situation; that he had every facility for doing in his caricatures.

found and allowed to assert their own native statement, they were treated with imaginative vision. In the Salon of 1824, Constable's *The Hay-Wain* was exhibited, while another contingent of English water-colourists was also there. *The Hay-Wain* caused a sensation. Delacroix painted out his *Massacre of Scio*, to start it again reinforced by what he had learned from Constable about technique—that a general appearance of one colour is composed with the aid of other contributory colours, which was to be a fundamental of impressionism. The landscape-painters of initiative also absorbed this addition to their science and the wider implication of *The Hay-Wain* as well. It might be exaggerating to say that from it they realised that the actual painting of the subject was more important than the subject itself; they were at any rate convinced that the quality of the picturesque was not an absolute to which only certain subjects could attain, but something to be educed from the subject itself. It was a more realistic romanticism than that which Delacroix and his followers applied to the story-picture, yet it was still romantic in its emphasis on the power of nature to express abstract moods, more literary than purely visual—such as nobility, tragedy or poetry. There remained the desire to paint the thing felt rather than the thing seen.

Beyond Constable, they found support for their aims in the Dutch landscape painters, and especially in Hobbema and Ruysdael. At not too great a distance from Paris the forest of Fontainebleau, in which they settled at the village of Barbizon, afforded them profuse material for the emulation of those masters. The Barbizon School is no longer as fashionable as it was half a century ago, yet a fine probity distinguished its productions and it did a greater service than is now always granted by encouraging the more purely visual approach of the painter to his theme.

One of its chief pioneers was Théodore Rousseau † (1812–1867), for long known as "The Great Rejected" from the regularity with which the official Salon refused to admit the works that he sent up from Barbizon. It is difficult now to realise the anger which they provoked, equal to the contumely bestowed on Delacroix. The latter, however, was able to set influential means at work to secure his exhibition, where Rousseau did not succeed until, without the Salon's aid, his painting forced its way to public esteem. He was the most prosaic, though the most powerful, member of the group, and it is likely that his refusal of forced effect and surface polish carried with it, to official eyes, the suggestion of a factual, democratic outlook which brought it into political disfavour. It is always extraordinary to what extremes and fantasies politics can be led if they mingle in matters of art. The jury of the official Salon of Rousseau's time had, in the exercise of its functions, the task of keeping sharp watch against the insinuation by means of paint of those new ideas which are always dangerous to an unsteady régime. His novelty, simply as an artist, was enough to make him potentially dangerous. Now, his faithfulness to nature and the honesty with which he recorded it, bring nothing exceptional with them; they are demanded of the merest journeyman of art. But his immense resourcefulness can still be admired. Every aspect of forest scenery finds him ready for its depiction and he wins something elemental to his work—a sense of the primaeval and the grandiose which is not factitious.

Ulysse Diaz (1808–1876) was the Barbizon painter most deeply and consciously imbued with the romantic doctrine. He began his career as a painter on porcelain, and this may have made some contribution to the brilliant glitter of his colour. It has been said that he would go into the forest with a palette already prepared with gleaming tints, and then pitch his easel in front of whatever scene he perceived to respond to them. The legend is a compliment to his achievement in restoring a lost freshness of line to landscape-painting. It helped to do away with the fetish of Hobbema's brown tree and the effect of spurious antique practised by the Salon tree-painters who slavishly imitated the Dutch masters. The flamboyance of Diaz's work may be attributed to his Spanish parentage; his dashing approach and virile brushwork are nearly related to the Spanish School; they are always consistently sustained and in keeping. It is a heightened colour-vision which conforms to its own logic and laws of relation.

Charles Daubigny (1817–1878) was not a member of the Barbizon group, though he may claim inclusion among them on account of his work being so deeply in sympathy with theirs and strongly influenced by it. The mood of his painting is tender and elegaic, seeking out the more intimate aspects of nature for its sensitive response. There is a sameness, yet not a monotony, about it, for the flow of the lesser rivers, which were his customary subject, gives it a continuous movement. His tranquil record of fact, unstirred by drama and with only the faintest heightening of romantic accent, arrests by its evident candour and its very lack of assumption.

A colony of painters, the nature of whose work is affiliated to that of Théodore Rousseau, established itself at Barbizon. While it cannot be ignored on account of the office it performed in bringing landscape-painting nearer to nature, it has rather the air of a quiet backwater in the history of French art. But the names of Camille Corot † (1796–1875) and Jean-François Millet ‡ (1814–1875) stand out from its somewhat parochial annals. They were of too great a magnitude to be enclosed within the boundaries of a coterie.

Corot, indeed, except for occasional revivals of the pure fire, had done his best work before he settled at Barbizon. There he fell into a poetic convention of painting which won vast popularity, but whose

† Plate 15   ‡ Plate 17

sentimentality has not stood the test of time. The feathery, generalised trees, the pool, and the suspicion of a band of disporting nymphs, are dainty and pretty, but of the weakest imaginative calibre, and at the same time a semi-detached gloss upon reality. Their manufacture may be excused for the francs that they permitted this most generous of painters to distribute in charity that included the support of Honoré Daumier's old age: yet that does not justify them as paintings.

And all the time of their production, Corot's early work, which proclaimed him one of the greatest of French painters and had been refused with annual regularity by the Salon, was lying undisturbed round the walls of his studio. These pictures were landscapes of Italy and the Midi of France, painted with the clear vision of a primitive and the exquisite instinct for handling the material of paint itself that Corot shared with Chardin. It is the custom at present to claim Corot as a classic, since that School is in favour for the time being and its label is a certificate of approval. Certainly, he was no romantic in his work that counts, while the later would-be lyric pieces were romanticism of an unfortunate kind. But the classical penchant for artifice and systematisation cast none of its blight upon his all-embracing acceptance of nature. He had, indeed, the feeling for order and distinctness of outline; but these were not necessarily a classical monopoly. On the other hand, while he was much more than a merely imitative realist, he allowed his subject the free possession of his scheme of design; he selected, and even slightly arranged, but always remained true to the elements as to the whole character of the scene, with no hint of idealisation. The subject preserves its own integrity in the picture. With the exception sometimes of Bonington (if he is to be claimed for France), Corot was the first French painter to let it do so.

His other innovation was volume: not even Cézanne himself was more attentive

in his rendering of third dimensional substance, which allowed him to pursue the penetration of light into the depths of the painting. It is usually the sunlight of full daytime, giving a radiance to that upon which it plays, intensifying though not altering colour. And Corot's colour is another of his tonic qualities, along with the compressed resilience of his form. Although capable of the utmost nicety, the finest shade, in its correspondence with this or that gradation of the details of the scene, there is nothing confused or disturbed about it. But with Corot all is limpid, innocent alike of over-stress and over-subtlety. It is painting of a Virgilian timbre, accomplished with a grave humility and communicating an enduring happiness.

His portraits have the same open mood, the same transparent honesty that yet reveals unexpected riches. His sitters are mostly studio-models, not particularly vivacious in expression, and frequently costumed in very perfunctory style as gitanas or contadinas. Still, Corot, with no departure from what is before him, no trouble to make the masquerade carry conviction or dramatise the unexciting pose, invests his representation with the tranced mellowness of a Giorgione. The unimpassioned figure takes on the aspect of a Sybil, the solidity is touched with majesty, and an abundance of pictorial incident, which only Corot could have educed from the appearance, is drawn to the unhurried completion of its chapter. Once Corot has shown that these possibilities were in his subject, we discover that such was indeed the case. It needed his capability of discerning in everything its precise pictorial aptitude to make them manifest. Where most vision is content with a factual summing-up of appearances, Corot simultaneously transposed them into elements of his art.

If, in his connection, the name of Virgil

is almost bound to occur, that of Homer comes, though more tentatively, in Millet's. He suggests an epic spaciousness: the figures of his labouring peasants seem to magnify themselves before one and to be engaged in toil stretching from the beginning to the end of the years. The awkwardness of their poses takes on a grandeur and dignity. Millet, as no other painter except Giotto, mingles simplicity of presentation with the sense of humanity. He did not "discover" the peasant, who had been made a figure of idyll or tragedy by other painters before him, but he was the first to show the peasant as he was, without adding a sentimental interpretation. There is nothing sentimental in *The Angelus* itself; the sentiment of that entirely matter-of-fact work is supplied by the spectator. The painfully-bent figures of *The Gleaners* may inspire pity for their deadening toil, but Millet does not demand it. If his work rouses strong feelings of identification with his subject, it is because the subject is stated with such complete bareness of pictorial truth that the spectator is impelled to cover it with his own emotion.

For Millet is a master of pictorial truth, which is largely a matter of artistic omission. Not to imitate, but to select and still give a satisfactory conception of the whole, is the painter's aim, and he carried out his excision of irrelevancies until his work has the large, free movement of primitive fresco, though lacking any suspicion of the archaic. His colour is vivid and almost raw, which helps the impression of earthiness. He had himself shared the life of his peasants. It may be that his experience of what he painted did its part in preserving him from decorative vagueness as from rhetorical sentiment—either of which an artist approaching Millet's themes from the outside might not so well have avoided, while the peasant, as a rule, is neither vague nor demonstrative about his labours.

In his painting he merely exercised the right to depict contemporary life as he viewed it, without restriction of material and down to the smallest detail if he wanted. In his series of caricatures entitled *Ancient History* he ridiculed the classicism which in his day still ruled the salon, by showing absurd modern figures in classical pose, some of them in picture-parody of David's own subjects. And although he was in sympathy with them against the common tyrant, his method of attack was applicable equally against the romantics with their insistence on dramatised emotion, and mediaevalism and exoticism. Daumier, in his paintings of the Paris and the Parisians of his day, was a founder of realism as a conscious movement in French art.

Gustave Courbet † (1819–1877) led it a step forward. He, again, was an artist of strong political convictions. A prominent member of the Paris Commune, he persuaded that Government, while it was in possession of the city, to demolish the Vendôme Column, which commemorated the triumphs of Napoleon. He objected to the monument both as a memorial to despotism and as an eyesore. Condemned to a fine which would pay for its re-erection, and imprisoned, when the Commune was repressed, he went to Switzerland, where he remained until his death.

Courbet spoke of himself as the painter of the social question, but, unlike David, he did not allow political propaganda to dominate his work. He claimed that *The Stone-breakers* and *Funeral at Ornans* were revolutionary in the feeling of social misery and injustice that they aroused, yet in themselves they are simply the straightforward representations of a peasant funeral and of two labourers at work. For Courbet's integrity as a realist did not permit him any tampering with the exact statement of the things he saw. He did not even attempt to suggest it by letting his own opinion or emotion create a cast of mood, or dwell expressively

† Plate 19

on some particular feature of the work. His people have no extra colouring of character, and in this respect he shows himself more ascetic than Daumier. The announcement of his first exhibition ran thus and no more: " Realism. G. Courbet. Exhibition of 40 of his Pictures." He had the right to proclaim himself the leader of the movement.

He held the show because the jury of the Universal Exhibition refused two of his most important works, *The Funeral at Ornans* and *The Studio*, for no other cause than that they gave an entirely natural rendering of their subjects. The régime was again unsteady, so again the official preference for art of an anodyne nature was enforced. But realism was in the air and irrepressible, entering literature and the drama, and, above all, suiting the tastes of a period when the rise of industrialism was creating a new public for it. From this public the classics still extracted lip-service; they had the sanction of official authority, but they touched no chord of popular sympathy. Romanticism appealed only in its debased melodramatic and ultra-sentimental forms : its higher flights appeared merely eccentric. Realism, however, which gave the public an unvarnished representation of the world it knew, without the necessity for classical and historical study to explain it, responded to the general if unvoiced demand. It could not be denied. Courbet's work might arouse a scandal, but at least it aroused interest, and, along with his own truculent self-assertion, made him a figure of popular notoriety.

This truculence is evident in his pictures, to their disadvantage. It tended to coarseness of treatment and frequent disregard of the elements of composition. That the subject should be painted as it is does not mean that simply to paint a thing as it is makes it a suitable subject. Courbet's larger works, containing a multitude of figures, fall to pieces because these figures have no pictorial connection, but only one of chance. They are an ill-assembled collection of portraits and passages of still-life or land-scape details, and though these in their isolation or uneasy juxtaposition may be brilliantly painted, they remain a gathering of scraps. *The Funeral at Ornans* unrolls like the old-fashioned panorama which showed one thing after another; a picture should join its sections together.

Courbet's landscapes are his most successful achievements, for there the continuity of nature, when needed, comes to his rescue and brings coherence. And once his rather hap-hazard choice of material offered him an opportunity, he could rise to it superbly. In colour, too, he was rarely at fault. Not only are the hues splendidly luminous and rich, and appropriate to the most transient weather-effect; their relations do not jar, as do the elements of his design. While he labours at the big effect, delightful smaller ones keep happening without his troubling about them.

Actually, within a much more limited range, Chardin had followed the tenets of realism as thoroughly as Courbet; but it was Courbet who made it a slogan, formulated its dogma, and launched it resoundingly as a movement. And his painting, as an example of it, held so much merit that any genuine artist who examined it without prejudice from a pro-fessional point of view was bound to admit that it was something more than a demon-stration of revolutionary politics; that there was a good deal to be learnt from it. The intelligent young painters of the bourgeoisie, even though they were warned that some-where vaguely in the background lurked a threat to the pillars of government, found much to learn from Courbet.

Henri Fantin-Latour † (1836–1904), whose very painting exhales a flavour of bourgeoisie, to whom Courbet's blustering manner both as a person and as a painter was antipathetic, yet made Courbet his master, discovering on the impetuously-filled acres of canvas a testimony to what, in the end, was just truth, and a satisfaction for his own sensitive, shy

† Plate 20

temperament. His pictures now seem a little dull, in spirit but not in colour. The large portrait-groups of his assembled friends, *Homage to Delacroix* and *The Dinner of the Poets*, assert rather pedantically his preferences in art and literature, yet there is courage in their quiet proclamation of his sympathy with the new Parnassian and Symbolist writers—even Rimbaud is admitted to the canvas—and with the rising school of Im-pressionist painters, who were far from having conquered general approval. Unlike Cour-bet's, his excellent portraiture is linked in well-arranged scheme when more than the single figure is involved. The very process of the painting gives pleasure—again an echo of Chardin. The flower-pieces, the ceaseless demand for which was sometimes lamented by Fantin-Latour himself, achieve a precision which, though respect-worthy, hardly moves, but the colour and quality of the pigment, its incrustation and lacquered richness, remain a delight.

Fantin's friend, Edouard Manet † (1832–1883), might be called, in the good sense of the epithet, the academic realist. It was his habit often to bring into his canvas supporting references to the old masters, pictorial quotations such as were used by Ingres, when he employed a detail from a Greek vase in his *Jupiter and Thetis*, and drew upon three different Madonnas by Raphael to compound the one of his own in *The Vow of Louis XIII*. Such adaptations were not copying, for the later men absorbed their loans into their individual style and perception. Manet in his best and non-impressionist work gave every inch of his canvas his altogether personal signature, in such things as the smooth and lucent texture of his paint, the luminosity of his blacks, and other painterly idiosyncrasies which make the personal style. The masters of the past whose works, or sections of whose works, he translated into his own idiom include Watteau, Chardin, Rubens, Rembrandt, Murillo, Velasquez and Zurbaran, to name

† Plates 21 and 22

outstanding examples. To particularise in two special cases, his *Déjeuner sur l'Herbe* draws for its conception and general plan from Giorgione's *Fête Champêtre*, and for the arrangement of its principal group from Marc Antonio's engraving after Raphael's *Judgment of Paris*, while the pose and major features of his *Olympia* come from Titian's *Venus of Urbino*.

Yet these pictures, dealing with two such hackneyed themes as a bathing-party and a recumbent nude, provoked the liveliest scandal. In vain Manet's few supporters invoked the general precedent and the example in detail of two of the most respectable of the old masters ; the fact that the old wine had been poured into a new bottle could not be tolerated. There was no objection to copies of the ancients, but that they should be modernised was the crime. The public objected to seeing something to which it had grown accustomed repeated in a new setting : it was not really clinging to morality, but to convention. Hostility died down as the works became gradually apprised from the standpoint of pictorial principles, when it was perceived that there was a good deal of classicism beneath their realistic surface, and that what Manet had done was to link up realism with the line of tradition.

Zola championed him zealously because he found Manet a convenient means of advancing his own doctrine of naturalism in literature, which considers all the phenomena of life worthy of description by the degree to which subject-matter is enlarged and the verisimilitude with which it is presented. Manet did not even take all of his subjects from life ; sometimes—as in the case of *Le Déjeuner sur l'Herbe* and *Olympia*—they are a deliberate studio-arrangement. But when he did care to paint the world about him, to indulge according to the right code of Courbet in the avowed realist manner which was the cause of so much alarm, the result was magnificent but singularly innocuous. Such crowded scenes, in which the whole canvas is filled with activity, as *Music at the Tuileries* or *The Bar of the Folies-Bergères*, not only catch the spirit of Second Empire and Third Republican Paris with an unerring ability of record, but gather up into their composition, which as a whole is sectional, with a simple direction of rhythm, a treasury of passages which have great formal interest of their own and yet create no disturbance in the prevailing unity.

Manet's portraits share with the separate figures of his Paris scenes something that can only be called an air. It is not character, or capable of analysis even, yet it is a property that distinguishes each individual from his fellows, and seems like an aura of his being. Manet netted it by a technical deftness, a sensitive response of his style to impalpables within the visual. It is evident, too, in his flower-pieces, in the folded roses and the glass vases from which they so triumphantly spring, where he seems along with the form to suggest something of the scent and an abstraction of transparency.

But with his constant and appreciative survey of the past and the contemporary in the craftsmanship of other artists, he became attracted to the rising Impressionist movement. In the work accomplished under its influence he lost much of his finer consistency without altogether obtaining the objects which impressionism indicated. It is significant that *The Bar of the Folies-Bergères* was a return to his earlier manner, made a short time before his death, and that it contains more power and reminiscence than the previous works of its kind. With all his splendid achievement behind him, Manet's greatest phase was arrested at its start.

IV. IMPRESSIONISM

THE new movement of impressionism in which Manet had experimented was a purely technical development of French art, unaccompanied by any implications, like the moral and psychological ones of classicism, romanticism and realism, outside the sphere of painting itself. Its practice can be traced back to Rubens and noted as part of the equipment of Watteau and Delacroix, who was reinforced in his use of it by the revelation of Constable. The impressionists themselves added a collateral ancestry, by way of Turner, from Claude.

The process of impressionism consisted in the breaking up of colour in agreement with the theory of complementary colours, according to which one of the primary colours—red, blue and yellow—needs the aid of the two others united into their secondary—green, orange or purple, respectively, of varying accent following the proportion of their components—in order that their proximity may heighten its own effect. There is thus an overlapping of colours throughout the whole picture, which results in the obliteration of precise boundaries of form; but it is instrumental in catching the more transient effects of light, and of bathing objects in light-filled atmosphere, while the loss of the pleasure of well-defined design is compensated by a greater effect of the harmony of colour relationship than was afforded with sharp limitations of line and the integrity of tints. In this respect the argument against impressionism becomes evident. It offers certain increased possibilities of representation, but at the expense of others; and in the various processes and issues of modern art which have developed from it the same weakening or disproportional value of some of the pictorial elements is involved. It is the exchange of a whole for a part; it seeks only a speciality of statement, yet that can be sufficient in itself.

The first conscious essay in impressionism as a modern movement was made, though tentatively, by Jongkind (1819–1891), a Dutch landscape and marine painter settled in France, whose moonlight scenes show an analytic investigation of the effect of certain conditions of light upon the objects on which they are exercised. This was carried further by his friend Eugène Boudin † (1824–1898) in his paintings of the port of Havre and its shipping, and of gay, crinolined groups of such holiday-makers as the Empress Eugènie and her suite at the coastal resorts of the neighbourhood. They most happily give the sensation of sunlight and fresh breezes and the movement of the sea, and in his work on them Boudin fulfilled one of the first qualifications of impressionism by painting in view of his subject, in the open air, instead of elaborating studies in his studio.

A younger artist from Paris, Claude Monet ‡ (1840–1926), often worked in his company, noting the advantages of his method in giving freshness and a convincing tang of weather to the canvas, though Boudin did not allow it to dim the clearness of his outline. Monet would not halt at such half-measures; he had no desire to attain, and also to stop short at, his friend's quiet, natty elegance. He wished to render with accuracy the appearance, exactly as he saw it, of objects out of doors; but at the beginning he could not claim full realisation of his aim, and was content to describe one of his experiments, in an exhibition catalogue, as an impression. From this came the name given by a satirical journalist to the movement.

Monet developed one technical aspect of realism. Vision, in the truth to it that he wanted to find the means of capturing, has no connection with the imagination; it is simply the act of seeing, and in order to record the result to a nicety, he trained himself in the art of perception. "Monet is all

† Plate 24   ‡ Plate 27

eye,—but what an eye !" said Cézanne, with grudging admiration. He was, indeed, as much a scientist in the pursuit of truth as an artist occupied with the creation of visual pleasure. An effect of light is of infinitely short duration, if, indeed, it is not in a state of continual alteration. To paint it accurately, it ought not to be rendered by a general synthesis of moments, but seized as nearly as possible in one moment. In order to preserve the unity of light of his picture, and to show its different variations, he worked at the same subject on different canvases at different times of the day. Thus he painted his series of cathedrals, haystacks, poplars and water-lilies. In them, as in his pictures of isolated subjects, he comes as near to mastery of the problem he sets himself as can be done without the mechanical means of colour-photography. It would not, however, be fair to say that all he does is to compete successfully with the camera, for he gives also the sense of the thought and enthusiasm of his effort, and the attraction of marvellous craftsmanship.

Alfred Sisley † (1840–1899) is very near to Monet as a purist of impressionism, though without the latter's occasional tinge of pedantry and intimation of the overcoming of difficulties. If weaker, he is more candid and humbler before the subject, approaching it with sympathetic insight rather than boldness of attack. While, like Monet, he troubled little about design, a poetry of mood gives unity to his picture, which, for all its sensitiveness, has a lively sparkle.

This happy gleam of vivacity quivers upon the surface of Sisley's landscapes with a lightheartedness that in the case of Camille Pissarro ‡ (1830–1903) is less demonstrative. Where Sisley is gay and perhaps a little superficial, Pissarro is tender and profound. He conveys atmosphere not only in the literal sense, but in that of spirit of place as well, and can conjure a subtlety of harmony from the most meagre of pictorial incident. Lacking the brilliance and excitement of his

fellow-impressionists, his graces do not leap to the eye, but, once discovered, they endure.

These painters, with Berthe Morisot † (1840–1895), Monet's sister-in-law, who painted delightful studies of girls and young women in sunshine, have much in common, seeking as they did the same result and attached to the rigid formula of the movement. There is a tension of experiment about their work, which combines with a bravery of adventure, though, ultimately, in the aim of painting nature's instant, they were attempting the impossible. Except for Monet, it is as much in the revelation of their own temperaments as in the approach to their imposed goal that the pleasure of their work consists.

Paul Cézanne ‡ (1839–1906) and Auguste Renoir (1841–1919) passed through impressionism to arrive each at his independent manner, calling for later consideration as post-impressionists. Edgar Degas § (1834–1917), the great urban representative of the movement, remained faithful to it until the end of his career, once it had won his adherence, though he considerably modified its tenets in his practice.

Degas came to impressionism from Ingres and the earlier Manet, and followed it in its main theory of the decomposition of colour and the search for the instantaneous effect, but working in his studio or in the evenly illuminated illusion of the theatre. The rendering of out-of-door atmosphere, with its special problem of light, did not affect him so deeply as it affected the landscape painters. This impressionism was rather one of form. He applied it chiefly to studies of the nude and of figurants of the Opera's ballet. In his pictures of the nude, although the theory of impressionism allows no admixture of a moral tendency, Degas introduced an attitude to life as surely as the landscape painters introduced their temperaments into their subjects. It was the point of view of a cynic who apparently enjoyed exposing the misery of humanity in the person of his models.

† Plate 25   ‡ Plate 23

† Plate 26   ‡ Colour Plate 4 and Plate 32
§ Colour Plate 3 and Plate 28

Starveling and bereft of physical attraction, they exhibit a variety of angular gesture, engaged at their toilet and their bath. Their own lack of approximation to any common notion of charm is made yet more manifest by the beauty which Degas gives in his oil paintings and pastels of them. Their movements are perfectly natural, yet Degas invests them with a quality of pattern suggestive of the Japanese artists of the colour-print, whose work he much admired. The colour, analysed into its contributory units, reaches extraordinary splendour.

In the theatre scenes he gets a magic of effect from the play of light upon the whiteness of the ballet-dancers' skirts, and the contrasted darkness and radiance of auditorium and stage. And here, too, his indefatigable draughtsmanship is displayed with astonishing ability in netting the poses of the dancers at practice and in the action of their stage performance. His race-course scenes are vivid with an intensity that equals Géricault's. But it is in the extremes of naturalism and artifice, in his nudes and ballet-dancers, that his greatness, which soon dispels the superficial appearance of virtuosity, is best asserted.

V. POST-IMPRESSIONISM

THE impressionists, because they had produced something new, were automatically disapproved of by public opinion and the conservative critics. The brunt of attack was directed against Paul Cézanne, who, because he was the most vigorous exponent of the movement rather than its most successful, was marked out as its representative. Monet, Sisley and Pissarro, while their work is fully quickened with vitality, display no violence. There is a sense of passionate effort about Cézanne's impressionism; and the most ardent of its adherents, he was the first to desert it in his restless search for self-expression.

Only by a dogged refusal to fail did he launch himself on a painter's career, having not only to overcome parental hostility, but the self-doubting that succeeded the bursts of impulse. Art was difficult, almost a torment, for him, though he could not abandon it. Until his last phase, his canvases denote toil and struggle. He had always the resource of colour, in his gift for applying it beautifully and wringing from it its last treasures of depth and glow, but for years he fumbled his drawing. Under the influence of Delacroix, he began by painting melodramatic fantasies on themes of orgy and assassination, followed by awkward adaptations of Manet's *Déjeuner sur l'Herbe* and *Olympia*. With these, however, went happier attempts at landscape and still-life, and on those subjects he concentrated under the tutelage of Pissarro, who initiated him into the impressionist method of painting directly from the subject and dividing his colour prismatically, by the use of which he achieved his first work of importance. Later his inclination towards solidity rather than surface got the upper hand, with the realisation, to put it at extremes, that the impressionists wanted to arrive at their subject while he wanted to enter into it. Leaving the mists of the Seine for the massive, keenly-outlined region of his native Provence, he at last found his way, and could exclaim, " I am painting as the almond-tree flowers."

Instead of using colour only as a film spread over the exterior of his subject, he made it denote the interior recessions of planes and analyse the theme into its component elements of form, whose volume he conveyed in a three-dimensional perspective. He not only, however, said, " All in nature is modelled upon the sphere, the cone and the

found and allowed to assert their own native statement, they were treated with imaginative vision. In the Salon of 1824, Constable's *The Hay-Wain* was exhibited, while another contingent of English water-colourists was also there. *The Hay-Wain* caused a sensation. Delacroix painted out his *Massacre of Scio*, to start it again reinforced by what he had learned from Constable about technique—that a general appearance of one colour is composed with the aid of other contributory colours, which was to be a fundamental of impressionism. The landscape-painters of initiative also absorbed this addition to their science and the wider implication of *The Hay-Wain* as well. It might be exaggerating to say that from it they realised that the actual painting of the subject was more important than the subject itself; they were at any rate convinced that the quality of the picturesque was not an absolute to which only certain subjects could attain, but something to be educed from the subject itself. It was a more realistic romanticism than that which Delacroix and his followers applied to the story-picture, yet it was still romantic in its emphasis on the power of nature to express abstract moods, more literary than purely visual—such as nobility, tragedy or poetry. There remained the desire to paint the thing felt rather than the thing seen.

Beyond Constable, they found support for their aims in the Dutch landscape painters, and especially in Hobbema and Ruysdael. At not too great a distance from Paris the forest of Fontainebleau, in which they settled at the village of Barbizon, afforded them profuse material for the emulation of those masters. The Barbizon School is no longer as fashionable as it was half a century ago, yet a fine probity distinguished its productions and it did a greater service than is now always granted by encouraging the more purely visual approach of the painter to his theme.

One of its chief pioneers was Théodore Rousseau † (1812–1867), for long known as " The Great Rejected " from the regularity with which the official Salon refused to admit the works that he sent up from Barbizon. It is difficult now to realise the anger which they provoked, equal to the contumely bestowed on Delacroix. The latter, however, was able to set influential means at work to secure his exhibition, where Rousseau did not succeed until, without the Salon's aid, his painting forced its way to public esteem. He was the most prosaic, though the most powerful, member of the group, and it is likely that his refusal of forced effect and surface polish carried with it, to official eyes, the suggestion of a factual, democratic outlook which brought it into political disfavour. It is always extraordinary to what extremes and fantasies politics can be led if they mingle in matters of art. The jury of the official Salon of Rousseau's time had, in the exercise of its functions, the task of keeping sharp watch against the insinuation by means of paint of those new ideas which are always dangerous to an unsteady régime. His novelty, simply as an artist, was enough to make him potentially dangerous. Now, his faithfulness to nature and the honesty with which he recorded it, bring nothing exceptional with them; they are demanded of the merest journeyman of art. But his immense resourcefulness can still be admired. Every aspect of forest scenery finds him ready for its depiction and he wins something elemental to his work—a sense of the primaeval and the grandiose which is not factitious.

Ulysse Diaz (1808–1876) was the Barbizon painter most deeply and consciously imbued with the romantic doctrine. He began his career as a painter on porcelain, and this may have made some contribution to the brilliant glitter of his colour. It has been said that he would go into the forest with a palette already prepared with gleaming tints, and then pitch his easel in front of whatever scene he perceived to respond to them. The legend

† Plate 18

is a compliment to his achievement in restoring a lost freshness of line to landscape-painting. It helped to do away with the fetish of Hobbema's brown tree and the effect of spurious antique practised by the Salon tree-painters who slavishly imitated the Dutch masters. The flamboyance of Diaz's work may be attributed to his Spanish parentage; his dashing approach and virile brushwork are nearly related to the Spanish School; they are always consistently sustained and in keeping. It is a heightened colour-vision which conforms to its own logic and laws of relation.

Charles Daubigny (1817–1878) was not a member of the Barbizon group, though he may claim inclusion among them on account of his work being so deeply in sympathy with theirs and strongly influenced by it. The mood of his painting is tender and elegaic, seeking out the more intimate aspects of nature for its sensitive response. There is a sameness, yet not a monotony, about it, for the flow of the lesser rivers, which were his customary subject, gives it a continuous movement. His tranquil record of fact, unstirred by drama and with only the faintest heightening of romantic accent, arrests by its evident candour and its very lack of assumption.

A colony of painters, the nature of whose work is affiliated to that of Théodore Rousseau, established itself at Barbizon. While it cannot be ignored on account of the office it performed in bringing landscape-painting nearer to nature, it has rather the air of a quiet backwater in the history of French art. But the names of Camille Corot † (1796–1875) and Jean-François Millet ‡ (1814–1875) stand out from its somewhat parochial annals. They were of too great a magnitude to be enclosed within the boundaries of a coterie.

Corot, indeed, except for occasional revivals of the pure fire, had done his best work before he settled at Barbizon. There he fell into a poetic convention of painting which won vast popularity, but whose

† Plate 15 ‡ Plate 17

sentimentality has not stood the test of time. The feathery, generalised trees, the pool, and the suspicion of a band of disporting nymphs, are dainty and pretty, but of the weakest imaginative calibre, and at the same time a semi-detached gloss upon reality. Their manufacture may be excused for the francs that they permitted this most generous of painters to distribute in charity that included the support of Honoré Daumier's old age: yet that does not justify them as paintings.

And all the time of their production, Corot's early work, which proclaimed him one of the greatest of French painters and had been refused with annual regularity by the Salon, was lying undisturbed round the walls of his studio. These pictures were landscapes of Italy and the Midi of France, painted with the clear vision of a primitive and the exquisite instinct for handling the material of paint itself that Corot shared with Chardin. It is the custom at present to claim Corot as a classic, since that School is in favour for the time being and its label is a certificate of approval. Certainly, he was no romantic in his work that counts, while the later would-be lyric pieces were romanticism of an unfortunate kind. But the classical penchant for artifice and systematisation cast none of its blight upon his all-embracing acceptance of nature. He had, indeed, the feeling for order and distinctness of outline; but these were not necessarily a classical monopoly. On the other hand, while he was much more than a merely imitative realist, he allowed his subject the free possession of his scheme of design; he selected, and even slightly arranged, but always remained true to the elements as to the whole character of the scene, with no hint of idealisation. The subject preserves its own integrity in the picture. With the exception sometimes of Bonington (if he is to be claimed for France), Corot was the first French painter to let it do so.

His other innovation was volume: not even Cézanne himself was more attentive

IV. IMPRESSIONISM

THE new movement of impressionism in which Manet had experimented was a purely technical development of French art, unaccompanied by any implications, like the moral and psychological ones of classicism, romanticism and realism, outside the sphere of painting itself. Its practice can be traced back to Rubens and noted as part of the equipment of Watteau and Delacroix, who was reinforced in his use of it by the revelation of Constable. The impressionists themselves added a collateral ancestry, by way of Turner, from Claude.

The process of impressionism consisted in the breaking up of colour in agreement with the theory of complementary colours, according to which one of the primary colours—red, blue and yellow—needs the aid of the two others united into their secondary—green, orange or purple, respectively, of varying accent following the proportion of their components—in order that their proximity may heighten its own effect. There is thus an overlapping of colours throughout the whole picture, which results in the obliteration of precise boundaries of form; but it is instrumental in catching the more transient effects of light, and of bathing objects in light-filled atmosphere, while the loss of the pleasure of well-defined design is compensated by a greater effect of the harmony of colour relationship than was afforded with sharp limitations of line and the integrity of tints. In this respect the argument against impressionism becomes evident. It offers certain increased possibilities of representation, but at the expense of others; and in the various processes and issues of modern art which have developed from it the same weakening or disproportional value of some of the pictorial elements is involved. It is the exchange of a whole for a part; it seeks only a speciality of statement, yet that can be sufficient in itself.

The first conscious essay in impressionism as a modern movement was made, though tentatively, by Jongkind (1819–1891), a Dutch landscape and marine painter settled in France, whose moonlight scenes show an analytic investigation of the effect of certain conditions of light upon the objects on which they are exercised. This was carried further by his friend Eugène Boudin † (1824–1898) in his paintings of the port of Havre and its shipping, and of gay, crinolined groups of such holiday-makers as the Empress Eugènie and her suite at the coastal resorts of the neighbourhood. They most happily give the sensation of sunlight and fresh breezes and the movement of the sea, and in his work on them Boudin fulfilled one of the first qualifications of impressionism by painting in view of his subject, in the open air, instead of elaborating studies in his studio.

A younger artist from Paris, Claude Monet ‡ (1840–1926), often worked in his company, noting the advantages of his method in giving freshness and a convincing tang of weather to the canvas, though Boudin did not allow it to dim the clearness of his outline. Monet would not halt at such half-measures; he had no desire to attain, and also to stop short at, his friend's quiet, natty elegance. He wished to render with accuracy the appearance, exactly as he saw it, of objects out of doors; but at the beginning he could not claim full realisation of his aim, and was content to describe one of his experiments, in an exhibition catalogue, as an impression. From this came the name given by a satirical journalist to the movement.

Monet developed one technical aspect of realism. Vision, in the truth to it that he wanted to find the means of capturing, has no connection with the imagination; it is simply the act of seeing, and in order to record the result to a nicety, he trained himself in the art of perception. " Monet is all

† Plate 24   ‡ Plate 27

outstanding examples. To particularise in two special cases, his *Déjeuner sur l'Herbe* draws for its conception and general plan from Giorgione's *Fête Champêtre*, and for the arrangement of its principal group from Marc Antonio's engraving after Raphael's *Judgment of Paris*, while the pose and major features of his *Olympia* come from Titian's *Venus of Urbino*.

Yet these pictures, dealing with two such hackneyed themes as a bathing-party and a recumbent nude, provoked the liveliest scandal. In vain Manet's few supporters invoked the general precedent and the example in detail of two of the most respectable of the old masters ; the fact that the old wine had been poured into a new bottle could not be tolerated. There was no objection to copies of the ancients, but that they should be modernised was the crime. The public objected to seeing something to which it had grown accustomed repeated in a new setting : it was not really clinging to morality, but to convention. Hostility died down as the works became gradually apprised from the standpoint of pictorial principles, when it was perceived that there was a good deal of classicism beneath their realistic surface, and that what Manet had done was to link up realism with the line of tradition.

Zola championed him zealously because he found Manet a convenient means of advancing his own doctrine of naturalism in literature, which considers all the phenomena of life worthy of description by the degree to which subject-matter is enlarged and the verisimilitude with which it is presented. Manet did not even take all of his subjects from life ; sometimes—as in the case of *Le Déjeuner sur l'Herbe* and *Olympia*—they are a deliberate studio-arrangement. But when he did care to paint the world about him, to indulge according to the right code of Courbet

in the avowed realist manner which was the cause of so much alarm, the result was magnificent but singularly innocuous. Such crowded scenes, in which the whole canvas is filled with activity, as *Music at the Tuileries* or *The Bar of the Folies-Bergères*, not only catch the spirit of Second Empire and Third Republican Paris with an unerring ability of record, but gather up into their composition, which as a whole is sectional, with a simple direction of rhythm, a treasury of passages which have great formal interest of their own and yet create no disturbance in the prevailing unity.

Manet's portraits share with the separate figures of his Paris scenes something that can only be called an air. It is not character, or capable of analysis even, yet it is a property that distinguishes each individual from his fellows, and seems like an aura of his being. Manet netted it by a technical deftness, a sensitive response of his style to impalpables within the visual. It is evident, too, in his flower-pieces, in the folded roses and the glass vases from which they so triumphantly spring, where he seems along with the form to suggest something of the scent and an abstraction of transparency.

But with his constant and appreciative survey of the past and the contemporary in the craftsmanship of other artists, he became attracted to the rising Impressionist movement. In the work accomplished under its influence he lost much of his finer consistency without altogether obtaining the objects which impressionism indicated. It is significant that *The Bar of the Folies-Bergères* was a return to his earlier manner, made a short time before his death, and that it contains more power and reminiscence than the previous works of its kind. With all his splendid achievement behind him, Manet's greatest phase was arrested at its start.

portraits and passages of still-life or land-scape details, and though these in their isolation or uneasy juxtaposition may be brilliantly painted, they remain a gathering of scraps. *The Funeral at Ornans* unrolls like the old-fashioned panorama which showed one thing after another; a picture should join its sections together.

Courbet's landscapes are his most successful achievements, for there the continuity of nature, when needed, comes to his rescue and brings coherence. And once his rather hap-hazard choice of material offered him an opportunity, he could rise to it superbly. In colour, too, he was rarely at fault. Not only are the hues splendidly luminous and rich, and appropriate to the most transient weather-effect; their relations do not jar, as do the elements of his design. While he labours at the big effect, delightful smaller ones keep happening without his troubling about them.

Actually, within a much more limited range, Chardin had followed the tenets of realism as thoroughly as Courbet; but it was Courbet who made it a slogan, formulated its dogma, and launched it resoundingly as a movement. And his painting, as an example of it, held so much merit that any genuine artist who examined it without prejudice from a pro-fessional point of view was bound to admit that it was something more than a demon-stration of revolutionary politics; that there was a good deal to be learnt from it. The intelligent young painters of the bourgeoisie, even though they were warned that some-where vaguely in the background lurked a threat to the pillars of government, found much to learn from Courbet.

Henri Fantin-Latour † (1836–1904), whose very painting exhales a flavour of bourgeoisie, to whom Courbet's blustering manner both as a person and as a painter was antipathetic, yet made Courbet his master, discovering on the impetuously-filled acres of canvas a testimony to what, in the end, was just truth, and a satisfaction for his own sensitive, shy

† Plate 20

temperament. His pictures now seem a little dull, in spirit but not in colour. The large portrait-groups of his assembled friends, *Homage to Delacroix* and *The Dinner of the Poets*, assert rather pedantically his preferences in art and literature, yet there is courage in their quiet proclamation of his sympathy with the new Parnassian and Symbolist writers—even Rimbaud is admitted to the canvas—and with the rising school of Im-pressionist painters, who were far from having conquered general approval. Unlike Cour-bet's, his excellent portraiture is linked in well-arranged scheme when more than the single figure is involved. The very process of the painting gives pleasure—again an echo of Chardin. The flower-pieces, the ceaseless demand for which was sometimes lamented by Fantin-Latour himself, achieve a precision which, though respect-worthy, hardly moves, but the colour and quality of the pigment, its incrustation and lacquered richness, remain a delight.

Fantin's friend, Edouard Manet † (1832–1883), might be called, in the good sense of the epithet, the academic realist. It was his habit often to bring into his canvas supporting references to the old masters, pictorial quotations such as were used by Ingres, when he employed a detail from a Greek vase in his *Jupiter and Thetis*, and drew upon three different Madonnas by Raphael to compound the one of his own in *The Vow of Louis XIII*. Such adaptations were not copying, for the later men absorbed their loans into their individual style and perception. Manet in his best and non-impressionist work gave every inch of his canvas his altogether personal signature, in such things as the smooth and lucent texture of his paint, the luminosity of his blacks, and other painterly idiosyncrasies which make the personal style. The masters of the past whose works, or sections of whose works, he translated into his own idiom include Watteau, Chardin, Rubens, Rembrandt, Murillo, Velasquez and Zurbaran, to name

† Plates 21 and 22

In his painting he merely exercised the right to depict contemporary life as he viewed it, without restriction of material and down to the smallest detail if he wanted. In his series of caricatures entitled *Ancient History* he ridiculed the classicism which in his day still ruled the salon, by showing absurd modern figures in classical pose, some of them in picture-parody of David's own subjects. And although he was in sympathy with them against the common tyrant, his method of attack was applicable equally against the romantics with their insistence on dramatised emotion, and mediaevalism and exoticism. Daumier, in his paintings of the Paris and the Parisians of his day, was a founder of realism as a conscious movement in French art.

Gustave Courbet † (1819–1877) led it a step forward. He, again, was an artist of strong political convictions. A prominent member of the Paris Commune, he persuaded that Government, while it was in possession of the city, to demolish the Vendôme Column, which commemorated the triumphs of Napoleon. He objected to the monument both as a memorial to despotism and as an eyesore. Condemned to a fine which would pay for its re-erection, and imprisoned, when the Commune was repressed, he went to Switzerland, where he remained until his death.

Courbet spoke of himself as the painter of the social question, but, unlike David, he did not allow political propaganda to dominate his work. He claimed that *The Stone-breakers* and *Funeral at Ornans* were revolutionary in the feeling of social misery and injustice that they aroused, yet in themselves they are simply the straightforward representations of a peasant funeral and of two labourers at work. For Courbet's integrity as a realist did not permit him any tampering with the exact statement of the things he saw. He did not even attempt to suggest it by letting his own opinion or emotion create a cast of mood, or dwell expressively

† Plate 19

on some particular feature of the work. His people have no extra colouring of character, and in this respect he shows himself more ascetic than Daumier. The announcement of his first exhibition ran thus and no more : " Realism. G. Courbet. Exhibition of 40 of his Pictures." He had the right to proclaim himself the leader of the movement.

He held the show because the jury of the Universal Exhibition refused two of his most important works, *The Funeral at Ornans* and *The Studio*, for no other cause than that they gave an entirely natural rendering of their subjects. The régime was again unsteady, so again the official preference for art of an anodyne nature was enforced. But realism was in the air and irrepressible, entering literature and the drama, and, above all, suiting the tastes of a period when the rise of industrialism was creating a new public for it. From this public the classics still extracted lip-service ; they had the sanction of official authority, but they touched no chord of popular sympathy. Romanticism appealed only in its debased melodramatic and ultra-sentimental forms : its higher flights appeared merely eccentric. Realism, however, which gave the public an unvarnished representation of the world it knew, without the necessity for classical and historical study to explain it, responded to the general if unvoiced demand. It could not be denied. Courbet's work might arouse a scandal, but at least it aroused interest, and, along with his own truculent self-assertion, made him a figure of popular notoriety.

This truculence is evident in his pictures, to their disadvantage. It tended to coarseness of treatment and frequent disregard of the elements of composition. That the subject should be painted as it is does not mean that simply to paint a thing as it is makes it a suitable subject. Courbet's larger works, containing a multitude of figures, fall to pieces because these figures have no pictorial connection, but only one of chance. They are an ill-assembled collection of in his rendering of third dimensional substance, which allowed him to pursue the penetration of light into the depths of the painting. It is usually the sunlight of full daytime, giving a radiance to that upon which it plays, intensifying though not altering colour. And Corot's colour is another of his tonic qualities, along with the compressed resilience of his form. Although capable of the utmost nicety, the finest shade, in its correspondence with this or that gradation of the details of the scene, there is nothing confused or disturbed about it. But with Corot all is limpid, innocent alike of over-stress and over-subtlety. It is painting of a Virgilian timbre, accomplished with a grave humility and communicating an enduring happiness.

His portraits have the same open mood, the same transparent honesty that yet reveals unexpected riches. His sitters are mostly studio-models, not particularly vivacious in expression, and frequently costumed in very perfunctory style as gitanas or contadinas. Still, Corot, with no departure from what is before him, no trouble to make the masquerade carry conviction or dramatise the unexciting pose, invests his representation with the tranced mellowness of a Giorgione. The unimpassioned figure takes on the aspect of a Sybil, the solidity is touched with majesty, and an abundance of pictorial incident, which only Corot could have educed from the appearance, is drawn to the unhurried completion of its chapter. Once Corot has shown that these possibilities were in his subject, we discover that such was indeed the case. It needed his capability of discerning in everything its precise pictorial aptitude to make them manifest. Where most vision is content with a factual summing-up of appearances, Corot simultaneously transposed them into elements of his art.

If, in his connection, the name of Virgil

is almost bound to occur, that of Homer comes, though more tentatively, in Millet's. He suggests an epic spaciousness: the figures of his labouring peasants seem to magnify themselves before one and to be engaged in toil stretching from the beginning to the end of the years. The awkwardness of their poses takes on a grandeur and dignity. Millet, as no other painter except Giotto, mingles simplicity of presentation with the sense of humanity. He did not " discover " the peasant, who had been made a figure of idyll or tragedy by other painters before him, but he was the first to show the peasant as he was, without adding a sentimental interpretation. There is nothing sentimental in *The Angelus* itself; the sentiment of that entirely matter-of-fact work is supplied by the spectator. The painfully-bent figures of *The Gleaners* may inspire pity for their deadening toil, but Millet does not demand it. If his work rouses strong feelings of identification with his subject, it is because the subject is stated with such complete bareness of pictorial truth that the spectator is impelled to cover it with his own emotion.

For Millet is a master of pictorial truth, which is largely a matter of artistic omission. Not to imitate, but to select and still give a satisfactory conception of the whole, is the painter's aim, and he carried out his excision of irrelevancies until his work has the large, free movement of primitive fresco, though lacking any suspicion of the archaic. His colour is vivid and almost raw, which helps the impression of earthiness. He had himself shared the life of his peasants. It may be that his experience of what he painted did its part in preserving him from decorative vagueness as from rhetorical sentiment—either of which an artist approaching Millet's themes from the outside might not so well have avoided, while the peasant, as a rule, is neither vague nor demonstrative about his labours.

III. REALISM

COROT and Millet lived and worked away from Paris, detached from the strife of opposed schools of painting and out of touch with contemporary events. Their pictures bear the imprint of no scholastic point of view and of no period, Corot's being concentrated exclusively on the abiding aspects of nature, Millet's overriding particularities with his compelling generalisation. They both died in the early years of the Third Republic, Corot having known six changes in the régime of France, and Millet five. These changes and the social evolution that accompanied them had not left other painters so untouched; while Honoré Daumier † (1808–1879) took an active part in bringing one of them about.

The best part of his existence was consumed in the ceaseless production of drawings for the comic journals, most of which were also organs of political parties. Daumier, himself a strong Radical, did much of his work for *Le Charivari*, a paper on the opposition side, to which he contributed a long series of caricatures attacking King Louis-Philippe and his Government. Savage in their intensity, despite suppression from time to time by the police, they made a deep effect on popular opinion. Yet while his merciless thrusts were appreciated, they were not wholeheartedly enjoyed. Their ruthlessness and the nearness in style of the grotesque to the macabre gave an uneasy shudder. For this refusal to tickle the public palate Daumier never reached high payment, producing his weekly masterpieces for a pittance.

" The fellow has something of Michelangelo under his skin," said Balzac when he saw one of Daumier's caricatures, and Daumier made no secret of the source to which he owed much of his plastic quality and force of line. He gave elasticity to the Michelangelesque design, translating it, as it were, into colloquial idiom, using it as a redoubtable weapon upon innumerable topics.

† Plate 16

In his flow of invention, which never ran diluted, it was Balzac himself whom he most resembled; his albums compose a pictorial *Comédie Humaine*. In one series he scourged the classicism of the Davidian school; in another, the machinery of the law; in another, the intrigue of the theatrical profession; and so on, until the France, or at any rate the Paris, of his time, lay dissected in every member by his scarifying analysis. His most mordant severities were directed against the bourgeoisie in general; but for the poor and the unclassed he has a sympathy whose expression is of poignant effect. In his flicks at vagabonds, mountebanks and old broken-down rogues there is something of affection. He assumes no pomposity of moral attitude.

In Daumier's painting, where his sympathies shine with equal clearness but the caricature takes on a darker and more tragic aspect, his master in form is still Michelangelo, though there are reminiscences of Rembrandt in the sudden light and the profundity of shadow. His backgrounds reveal him as one of the most successful interpreters of the spirit of Paris as displayed in its urban landscape, the individuality of the quays and bridges of the Seine, the grey unity of façades and the desolation of outer suburbs, completing the emotional implication of his scene as a whole. Sometimes he adds ferocity to a subject from Molière, sometimes a quaintness to the fantasy of Cervantes, though most of the paintings are contemporary and realistic in theme and treatment.

It was a realism of character and of incident without anecdote. Though it is plain that Daumier could have felt himself in close relationship with his old print-hunters on the quays, his heroic working-women or his carriage full of third-class passengers, he does not arrange his facts into a situation; that he had every facility for doing in his caricatures.

Plate 3

Luxembourg, Paris

THE DANCER   By Edgar DEGAS (1834-1917)

cylinder ", but also, " To paint after nature is not to copy the objective, it is to realise one's sensations ", and while with an ascetic economy he condensed the expression of substance, he assigned to each of his modulations of tone a constructive function which was orchestral and architectural. Favouring the classic balance of design, he gave it a rhythmic force, which absorbs into its organism figure, landscape and still-life with an equal intensity. For, to quote him again, " Painting has no goal but itself ", and he permits no hint on the canvas that the human model makes in him any emotion of a different kind than that which he received from the mountain of Saint-Victoire or a bowl of apples.

His colour became more limpid and filled with light as he went on, with one particular shade of blue as characteristic of him as another, deeper one, was of Poussin, and on viewing some of his pictures, it seems as though his whole theory of form was but a mechanism for the exercise of his colour-sense.

The resolute inhumanity of Cézanne's work is altogether in contrast with that of Auguste Renoir † (1841–1919), who grew out of impressionism as the robust sensuality of his painting increased. Renoir began as a painter of porcelain, and the glitter and sharp outlines of that craft cling to his early canvases. Realising, however, the more modulated and fluid effect to be obtained from impressionism, he attached himself to the movement, soon to become one of its most expert adherents, evolving exquisite refinements of lustrous colour and showing great aptitude for imparting a tactile quality to his rendering of fabrics, such as apparel, upholstery or furs. In these first phases of his activity he found many of his subjects in the life of the Paris faubourgs with their vivacious, pretty working-girls, whom he depicted bustling about the Paris streets, at the theatre and on holiday outings.

Though they are not anecdotal, and convincingly confine themselves to the thing seen, these pictures are happy and sentimental

† Frontispiece and Plate 31

in tone, for Renoir took a cheerful view of life. In his portrait groups he appreciatively displays the dappled comfort of bourgeois interiors. For such a purpose, with its registration of the varied sheen of rich stuffs, impressionism admirably served the needs, but he grew, like Cézanne, to desire a greater solidity, the more so as his conceptions became more primitive, and, whether the figures were nude or clothed, flesh, glowing with health and abundant, became his dominant theme. For him, too, it was not the play of light, but the object on which it played that he wished in the first place to portray in its fullness of substance. And while he kept, on its broad lines, to the theory of divided colour to give the appearance of being bathed in sunlight to his female figures, he endowed them at the same time with a massive plastic quality. Like Cézanne, he had gone to live in the Midi, where the light held fewer subtleties and the atmosphere did not mute the full resonance of colour. There, in the peacock tints of his landscapes, the bright burnish of his roses, but chiefly in the hot fleshly vividness of his lusciously-rounded women and girls, he embodied his vision of primitive, natural plenty.

This later work of Renoir does not admit of adaptation, which could do little but imitate, but from his earlier period, and particularly from the interior-settings of his portraits, rose an off-shoot of impressionism known as Intimism, of which the two most prominent representatives are Pierre Bonnard † (born 1867) and Edouard Vuillard (1868–1940). Bonnard has the palette of wider range and is a true inventor in colour, but his design is more diffuse than Vuillard's. They both give delightful glimpses of Paris, its streets and gardens, but more especially of its high-bourgeois interiors, which became jewelled coruscations at their hands. While seeking only to seize the charm of a tangled wealth of interwoven tones, they convey the social atmosphere of a period and a class described in the novels of Paul Bourget.

† Plate 36

This is done with intention by Henri de Toulouse-Lautrec † (1864–1902), who closely followed Degas in his technique of impressionism and devoted it for the most part to presenting the agents and patrons of the pleasures of Montmartre towards the end of the century. He was a brilliant draughtsman and illustrative reporter, but his paintings, for all their mordant liveliness of observation, suffer, unlike his excellent posters and lithographs, from muddiness of colour.

After impressionism, French painting of a progressive nature becomes preoccupied with technical problems, less representational and more detached from its environment. Georges Seurat ‡ (1859–1891), besides his pictures of the Normandy coast, painted circus scenes and Parisian river-resorts, but their greater interest is their method of execution. The drawing is very exact in its simplification, and there is something of suspended motion in the forms that reminds one of Ingres; they catch and guard their instant in a superb rightness of design. Seurat tried, indeed, to find a way by which reason might accomplish the work of instinct and capture the evanescent moment with a theory of optics, on which he wrote a treatise. He attempted a precise registration of his colour, but instead of the component tints being put on the canvas in a hurried labour of dabs and streaks, he applied them in small confetti-like pointings of nicely-calculated gradation of size and hue from prepared studies. But in the end it was instinct that gave to his invention a success which its other practitioners have failed to achieve.

One of them was Vincent van Gogh § (1853–1890), a Belgian who worked the greater part of his painting life in France. He tried impressionism and Seurat's pointillism in a desperate effort to find a work of expression that would fit him, but the most enduring influence on him was that of the Japanese colour-print, then a new discovery. His paint has a lacquer-blue consistency and clearness, and in its application testifies to the same intensity that marks the dynamic quality of rhythm in his design. While he accomplished his most powerful work he was tormented by religious disquiet, poverty and the fear of falling short of his aspirations in art. His distress left its sign upon his painting, which is poignant with the sharpest moods of escape into elation and relapse into despair.

Van Gogh was closely associated with Paul Gauguin † (1848–1903), with whom he quarrelled in a fit of nervous irritation that was a prelude to his lunacy and suicide. As a disciple of Degas, Gauguin had gone through an impressionist period, and, like Van Gogh, greatly admired Japanese colour-prints. But he was susceptible to innumerable influences, which also included the Florentine masters, Breton calvaries and Papuan sculpture. These he welded into a decorative system by which he mostly painted Breton landscape, until the desire to find a reality which would approach his exotic imaginings led him to Tahiti, where he died. His Tahitian landscapes and subject-pictures are painted in his decorative style, which he deeply tinged with a formalisation of his surroundings. Impressionism has altogether disappeared in favour of unmingled colour, and the whole scene is brought evenly to the surface in a flatness of pattern, without distance of approach or recession. An atmosphere of mysticism distils in the painting the sentiment of the contemporary school of symbolist poets, on whom Gauguin and his work had considerable influence.

Gauguin's painting, with its mingled atmosphere of savagery and dreaminess, was very different from the kind of decoration sponsored by the official bodies which called upon prize-winning artists of the Salons to cover the walls of public buildings. The importance of such works was considerable, for large sections of the people, who set foot neither in the Louvre nor in contemporary exhibitions, to whom impressionism and the

† Plate 30   ‡ Plate 33   § Plate 34   † Plate 35

battle of movements in art were things unknown, found their only picture-gallery in those edifices. The mural painters controlled popular taste and mostly gave it an emptily-grandiose pictorial convention, into which were poured the clichés of false sentiment and second-rate poetry, to browse upon.

There was, however, one exception, Pierre Puvis de Chavannes † (1824–1898), who, by the subterranean exercise of social privilege, managed to obtain possession of a large amount of municipal wall-space, and for forty years, until the end of the century, serenely self-confined within his own imaginative vision, executed work that was worthy of its place of showing. He counted, incidentally, among the many influences upon Gauguin, while he himself learnt much from the Italian primitive fresco-painters and from Botticelli. But he introduced a modern note into his figures, whose emaciation suggests a too-definite urban characteristic of contemporary life as much as Florentine grace, stressed as it is by the deliberate angularity of Puvis's manner of presenting gesture. Picasso, in his early work, has caught some suggestions from it.

Puvis's design was severely simplified, with a knowingness of naivety, flatly two-dimensional; his colour subdued, yet unsensationally sure in its effect. The whole scheme is uncrowded, single figures and small groups carrying out the necessary dramatic suggestion, which, despite a certain bareness, does just fill the space. This he peopled with saints, nymphs, shepherds, warriors and all the imaginable stock personages of legend and allegory, yet they keep a pictorial verisimilitude in their poetic remoteness, possibly on account of his method of transposing, when it would serve his purpose, much of what he actually perceived into his fiction. A group of trees would come from a landscape that he knew, a group of children he transposed from the life; he did not offer the usual bogus convention.

VI. THE FREEDOM OF FORM

CEZANNE, when he said that the aim of painting was not to copy the objective, but to realise one's sensations, defined the trend of progress in French art for the period that has followed impressionism. The artists have used the appearance, whether existing in reality or in their imagination, to express their feelings about it, but not to reproduce it, or to create for the spectator the illusion of its existence. Its function has stopped short at suggesting to them, and usually providing them, with the elements of form for their expression.

The spectator who compares the resultant picture with his own idea of its subject is unjust in condemning it if the two do not agree. It is said that the possession of what is scientifically known as normal vision is an abnormality, and though for practical purposes there is general consent as to the main characteristics of form and colour in an object, different beholders' visions of them are considerably varied round about the common factor of consent, the " by and large " of it. With the lack of attempts to teach the art of seeing, there are many who, unless there is special need of observation, more or less ignore the aspects of their environment. Yet they would not hesitate to judge a picture from the point of view of their inadequate visual experience, when the artist, an expert at the job of looking at things, is asking them to do so from the point of view of his, which has in every case been directed upon something other than imitation. Modern art is too often lumped in general disapproval because the spectator insists upon ignoring its intention.

† Plate 29

The ways in which this intention may be fulfilled are as many as the artists themselves, and sometimes an individual artist is not consistent in the use of a single way, just as a writer alters his style, or produces now a comedy, now a tragedy. Pablo Picasso † (born 1881) is disconcerting even to his admirers by the variety of his methods and moods. When he first arrived in Paris from Spain, his work resembled Toulouse-Lautrec's. Ingres and Puvis influenced exquisite early groups of acrobats and nomads and boys leading horses, painted in dominant keys of blue and pink, while some of his early figure-studies are tinged with tragic and humanitarian implications that did not again appear in his work until his republican sympathies in the Spanish Civil War led to the tragic symbolism of his *Guernica*. Most of his work, however, is as abstract in the joy of its expression as Cézanne's, though before the war he had begun, as an accredited surrealist, to depict the images of his subconscious fantasy. Of his many adventures in formal experiments, the most notable is cubism, to which, under various modifications, he has intermittently returned.

Starting from Cézanne's dissection of his subject into its three-dimensional elements of form, based upon the geometric types of volume, cubism with those constructs a design which, unlike Cézanne's, need not include them all or combine them again in their natural order. It may be satisfied with only enough of them to suggest the appearance, which is the picture's point of departure instead of its goal. It may juxtapose, or impose upon each other, the representation of those elements presented from more than one view-point at the same time, on the same canvas.

The picture is thus confined to the essence of the subject itself, without count of light or the containing space, or even vista of perspective; it offers a simultaneous, one might say a fourth-dimensional, view of such different aspects of the subject at once as the

† Plate 42

design cares to accommodate. It frees form from the arbitrary mould of the appearance which contains it, to which the colour of the picture can correspond, or from which it can depart in order to build up its independent discord of harmony. It is a method capable of infinite development, and Picasso, with equal success, has applied it to landscape, figure and still-life. Yet the most impressive exponent of its resources is Georges Braque † (born 1881), who mainly confines himself to small still-lifes of fruit and a restrained scale of colour, exquisite in texture and application, from which he extracts inexhaustible variations.

Form was freed in another direction by Les Fauves, the Wild Men of painting, as they were called, whose aim was to give a visual impression of their subject which should convey especially its properties of colour, often deliberately emphasised, and of atmosphere, in the sense of mood. Frequently form is treated by them in a rudimentary, truculent manner, detail being swept away in order to reach the wider aspect of design, or simplified, with a free gesture of arabesque draughtsmanship, to the requisites for producing mood and colour effects. To obtain those with the greatest possible directness, a naivety of execution has been adopted, with conscious reminiscence of children's paintings and of primitive art. The Fauves have matured with time, and in some cases have become less lively, but their best production is stamped with the ardour and sense of liberation that distinguished their early common effort.

André Derain (born 1880) is the classic of the movement, even when, from the influence of negro sculpture, it is an African classicism. His form is selective, but firm and resolutely true to the appearance, and his colour, since his period of Fauvism, grave and robust; his tendency becomes more and more academic.

Henri Matisse ‡ (born 1860) attains radiant modulations of colour, and a tenuous but

† Plate 39   ‡ Plate 37

elastic design which is the final summary of his subject's lyrical properties. Amadeo Modigliani † (1884–1920), as much influenced by negro sculpture as were David and Ingres by that of Greece and Rome, drew his portraits and figure-studies in circular formal design, which, with extreme economy of delineation, yet preserve salient character and strong plastic value. Maurice Utrillo ‡ (born 1883), in the landscape of his native Parisian region of Montmartre, gives, with a dominant key of luminous grey, a poignant sense of spirit of place.

The work accomplished during the key day of Fauvism bears signs of an exultant anarchy, an enthusiastic kicking over of the traces. It was utterly independent of tradition, and though a great deal of labour went to selection of detail and establishment of harmony, it was necessary that the result should seem as spontaneous and unlaboured as possible, in order to leave the impression of a natural, unsophisticated approach to the subject. In Henri Rousseau § (1844–1910) a painter was discovered who seemed to fulfil this condition. He was a pensioned customs-house officer, whose Sundays off had for long been devoted to art. With his clarity of line and colour went that of a vision unshadowed by influences, and he had quietly worked away without instruction or encouragement until the poet and critic, Guillaume Apollinaire, came by chance upon him and introduced to the young painters of the day a surprising series of views of the Paris suburbs, still-lifes, family-groups and imaginary scenes of jungle and desert, some of which were souvenirs of the artist's experiences in Mexico as a soldier in the army sent out to support the unfortunate Emperor Maximilian. They were recognised at once as the productions of a temperament unsullied by the training of the schools, and at the same time of a very genuine instinct for painting.

The establishment of Rousseau's reputation was something of a joke, but its endurance is entirely serious. There is a comic element in the naivety of his surrender to his vision, especially in some of his imaginary scenes, but his rendering of it is altogether serious. A professional painter could only arrive at it by casting off what he had learned with as much labour as he had taken to acquire it. And Rousseau was more conscious of his gifts than he was always given credit for being. When a proposal was set on foot for collecting a fund to enable him to attend the studio-classes, he refused it with the remark that he knew exactly what he was doing in his painting, and preferred to continue as he was. His freshness, indeed, astonished, but with it goes a knowledge of his own; and his composition, most of all in his more patterned work, is as masterly as his observation; his recognition of what makes a picture is delightful. Rousseau is a natural classic, and at the same time the first modern master of proletarian art. In his feeling for line and orderly form, nothing in French painting had been achieved so near in spirit to Poussin and Ingres since the latter's death. But while he in isolation was reviving a lost integrity of form and impassiveness of style, another independent, Georges Rouault,† was filling his work with an intensity of emotion only equalled hitherto, in their very different manners, by Grunewald, Rembrandt and Goya.

Rouault was the pupil of Gustave Moreau, a mystical painter who sought jewelled effects but rarely achieved more than tinsel. Rouault is religious, but not mystical, and the sense of tragedy which he brings to his sacred subjects takes on a savagely satiric tinge in his paintings of real life, in which, for example, he invests the tribe of the law with a horror far exceeding Daumier's. The one institution that finds sympathy from him is the circus, brutal and coarse in its spangled garishness, to which he adds a lustre, yet robustly jovial and with something dynamic in its tawdry grandeur. His landscapes, snatches of urban outskirts, are heavy with sombre desolation. With a

† Plate 43   ‡ Plate 38   § Plate 40   † Plate 44

tendency to enclose his forms in thick black outline, recalling its leaden setting, one discerns in his pictures a likeness to stained glass with its gleam of smouldering colours irradiating the darkness of a Romanesque cathedral. Rouault stands alone in French painting for his gloom and splendour, his tragedy and farce, yet, as it is French painting, these properties are disciplined with a force of concentration that redoubles their significance.

Some painters from abroad have so identified themselves with the art-life of Paris, like Picasso, that they count as French painters, and one of them, the Russian Soutine, in his still-lifes of dead fowls and flamboyant chunks of meat, and still more in his contorted landscapes and portraits tilted strongly towards caricature, has some affinity, while keeping his individuality in the fantastic, with Rouault.

Marc Chagall,† also a Russian, paints his native folk-lore and his dreams in rich, bright colours whose texture increases the pleasure of their genuine fairy-tale feeling. He is not officially included in the surrealist association, perhaps because his subconscious is not self-conscious enough, yet his dream-pictures ring truer in their lyrical simplicity than some of the more elaborate treatments of the same theme by recognised members of the movement.

What was at first the personal, and even automatic, record of the imagery released in a mind over which the control of reason had been voluntarily suppressed—the original surrealist picture—has evolved into a new romanticism. Unlike the old one, it does not go to the past or to remote countries for its subject-matter, but finds it rather in the symbolic representation of personal moods and an imaginative contemporary life. Its transposition of tendency is towards the

† Plate 41

whimsical or the macrabre. When the shock of its unconventional enlargement of pictorial subject has worn off, and it is judged purely on its achievement as art, its inventive fertility and its revival of skilled draughtsmanship and architectural composition will claim due esteem. At present the pathological element of surrealist painting, in its interpretation of individual and general neurosis, tends to distract attention from such strictly pictorial qualities, particularly when the artist exploits it as a sufficient substitute for them.

Degas, whose work suggests a decided attitude to life, delivering, as it went on, the summing-up without illusion of a long experience, insisted that pictures were made with paint, and not with ideas. The assertion seems at first a platitude, but in its implications it points to the especial achievement of French art. In the mental approach to their subject, and often in the choice of it, the great painters of France have shown themselves in accord with the intellectual progress of their time, usually first marked in literature and soon of European acceptance. Their originality consists less in the conception than in the method of its expression. Here, for over a century, French painting has taken the lead, engaging on constant experiment in the expansion of its technique, bringing to the canvas aspects of appearances that hitherto were unrecorded. This endeavour, so long sustained by native qualities of reason and courage, has not only nourished the science of the art; for those who view the result, it enlarges the capacity of vision. France has bestowed upon the world many gifts of the spirit; the continuance of this adventurous tradition in her painting comes early in the hope—the need—for a resumption of her bounty.

BIBLIOGRAPHY

BASLER, A.
    Henri Rousseau (Paris, 1927).

BELL, CLIVE
    An Account of French Painting (London, 1928).
    Since Cézanne (London, 1924).

BLANCHE, JACQUES-EMILE
    Les Arts Plastiques (Paris, 1931).

CEZANNE, PAUL
    Letters (London, 1943).

DELACROIX, EUGÈNE
    Journal (Paris, 1893).

DURET, T.
    Les Peintres Impressionistes (Paris, 1936).

FRY, ROGER
    Characteristics of French Art (London, 1932).

GAUGUIN, PAUL
    Intimate Journals (London, 1930).

JAMOT et WILDENSTEIN
    Manet (Paris, 1932).

LAPAUZE, H.
    Ingres, sa vie et son oeuvre (Paris, 1911).

MAGNE, E.
    Nicolas Poussin, premier peintre du Roi (Brussels, 1914).

STEIN, GERTRUDE
    Picasso (London, 1938).

THOMSON, D. C.
    The Barbizon School of Painters (London, 1890).

VALERY, PAUL
    Degas (Paris, 1938).
    Pieces sur l'Art (Paris, 1934).

VAN GOGH, VINCENT
    Letters to his brother Theodore (London, 1927).

VOLLARD, AMBROISE
    En écoutant Cézanne, Degas, Renoir (Paris, 1938).

WILENSKI, R. H.
    Modern French Painters (London, 1940).

WILDENSTEIN, G.
    Chardin (Paris, 1933).

SOME EARLIER WORKS BY T. W. EARP

Flower and Still-Life Painting.   *Augustus John.*
Van Gogh.   *The Modern Movement in Painting.*

LIST OF PLATES

IN FULL COLOUR

MONOCHROME (Photogravure)

MONT Ste. VICTOIRE *By Paul Cézanne* (1839-1906)

Plate 4

BACCHANALIAN DANCE   *By Nicholas POUSSIN (1594–1665)*

Plate 5

Plate 6

MARRIAGE OF ISAAC AND REBECCA By CLAUDE LORRAIN (1600–1682)

FÊTE IN A PARK By Antoine WATTEAU (1684–1721)

Plate 7

Plate 8

STILL LIFE *By Jean-Baptiste-Siméon* CHARDIN (1699–1779)

Plate 9

ELIZA BONAPARTE, GRAND DUCHESS OF TUSCANY   *By Jacques-Louis DAVID* (1748–1825)

Plate 10

MME. RIVIÈRE   *By Jean-Auguste-Dominique* INGRES (1780–1867)

Plate 11

THE BARON SCHWITER *By Ferdinand-Victor-Eugène* DELACROIX (1798–1863)

DANTE'S BARQUE By Ferdinand-Victor-Eugène DELACROIX (1798–1863)

Plate 12

Plate 13

CAUGHT BY THE TIDE   By Jean-André-Théodore GERICAULT (1791–1824)

Plate 14

SCENE IN NORMANDY   *By Richard BONINGTON* (1802–1828)

National Gallery

Plate 15   THE CLAUDIAN AQUEDUCT   By Jean-Baptiste-Camille COROT (1796–1875)

Plate 16

THE THIRD-CLASS COMPARTMENT *By Honoré DAUMIER* (1808–1879)

Plate 17

THE WOOD SAWYERS   By Jean-François MILLET (1814–1875)

SUNSET IN THE AUVERGNE By Pierre-Etienne-Théodore ROUSSEAU (1812–1867)

Plate 18

THE STORM   *By Gustave* COURBET (1819–1877)

Plate 19

MR. AND MRS. EDWARDS *By Ignace-Henri-Jean-Théodore* FANTIN-LATOUR (1836–1904)

Plate 21

MLLE. EVA GONZALES *By Edouard MANET (1832–1883)*

Plate 22

DEJEUNER SUR L'HERBE   By Edouard MANET (1832–1883)

Louvre

C. Pissarro

Plate 23

AVENUE DE L'OPERA   By Camille PISSARRO (1830–1903)

Plate 24

THE BEACH, TOURGEVILLE   By Eugène-Louis BOUDIN (1824–1898)

Plate 25

WINTER   By Alfred SISLEY (1840–1899)

Plate 26

LE CHAMPS DE MARS *By Berthe* MORISOT (1840–1895)

Plate 27

POPLARS ON THE EPTE *By Claude-Oscar* MONET (1840–1926)

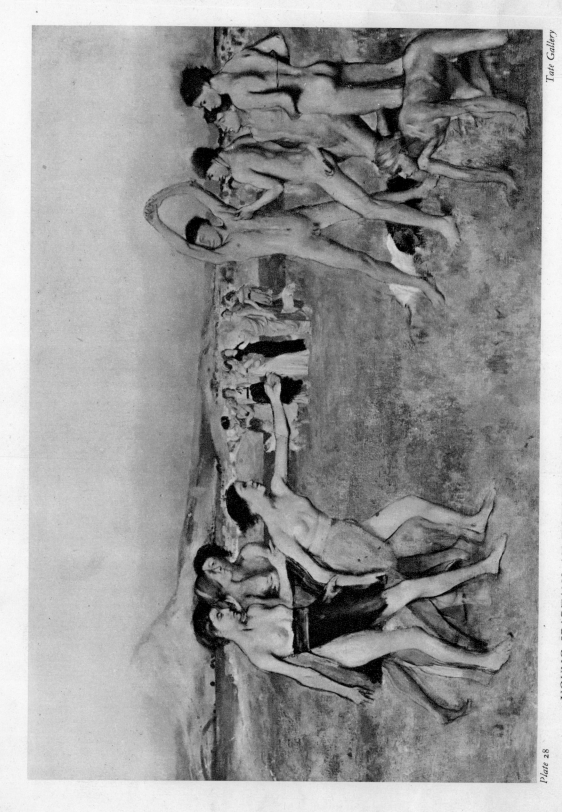

Plate 28

YOUNG SPARTANS AT WRESTLING PRACTICE   *By Hilaire-Germain-Edgar DEGAS (1834–1917)*

Tate Gallery

SUMMER   By Pierre-Cecile PUVIS DE CHAVANNES (1824–1898)

Plate 29

Plate 30

SEATED WOMAN *By Henri de TOULOUSE-LAUTREC (1864–1902)*

Plate 31   Sir Kenneth Clark

THE BLONDE BATHER   By Pierre-Auguste RENOIR (1841–1919)

Plate 32

BATHERS IN A LANDSCAPE   By Paul CEZANNE (1839–1906)

Plate 33   THE BATHING PLACE *By Georges-Pierre SEURAT (1859–1891)*

Plate 34

Photo.: *Lefevre Gallery*

BRIDGE AT ARLES By *Vincent VAN GOGH* (1853–1890)

Plate 35

NEVERMORE   *By Paul* GAUGUIN (1848–1903)

Plate 36

THE WINDOW   *By Pierre BONNARD* (1867)

Plate 37

WINDOW IN NICE *By Henri MATISSE* (1869)

Plate 38

THE PARK GATE   *By Maurice UTRILLO* (1883)

Photo. : Lefevre Gallery

Plate 39

POT AND GUITAR   *By Georges BRAQUE* (1881)

Plate 40

BICÊTRE   *By Henri ROUSSEAU* (1844–1910)

THE POET RECLINING *By Marc CHAGALL* (1887)

Plate 42

LIFE By *Ruiz Pablo* PICASSO (1881)

Plate 43

Tate Gallery

PORTRAIT OF A GIRL   *By Amedeo* MODIGLIANI (1884–1920)

Plate 44

CHRIST AND THE DOCTOR *By Georges* ROUALT (1871)